Through the Wilderness of
ALZHEIMER'S

Through the Wilderness of
ALZHEIMER'S
A Guide in Two Voices

ROBERT & ANNE SIMPSON

Augsburg
MINNEAPOLIS

To Alzheimer's patients everywhere and to the families
and communities that care for them

Proceeds from the sale of this book will be donated to support programs and services for Alzheimer's patients in Cook County, Minnesota.

Library of Congress Cataloging in Publication Data
Simpson, Robert, 1933–
    Through the wilderness of Alzheimer's: a guide in two voices/
Robert and Anne Simpson.
        p. c.m.
    Includes bibliographical references.
    ISBN 0-8066-3891-5 (alk. paper)
    1. Alzheimer's disease—Patient's Biography. I. Simpson, Anne, 1935– .
II. Title.
RC523.2.S56 1999
362.1'96831'0092
[B]—DC21   99-15969
                                                                            CIP

The paper used in this publication meets the minimum requirements of American National Standard for Information Sciences—Permanence of Paper for Printed Library Materials, ANSI Z329.48-1984.

Manufactured in the U.S.A.   AF 9-3891

03   02   01   3   4   5   6   7   8   9   10

CONTENTS

ACKNOWLEDGMENTS

This is our story, Bob's and mine. But the book is not only ours—it has taken on a life of its own through the labor and love of many others.

Jill Breckenridge and Margot Fortunato Galt helped us to conceive of such a serious writing project. If it were not for them, my notebooks would be stacked neatly in the bottom of my desk, gathering dust until children or grandchildren discovered them after my death.

Gary Atwood gave form to our words, laying out copy, patiently arranging and rearranging it, staying calm as deadlines approached, even when we fueled him with "North Shore Plasma" (strong black coffee).

Gail Irwin critiqued the writing, nurtured our dreams, and constantly reminded us to keep this journey in a spiritual perspective. So did Ann Wahlers, John Hogenson, and Dave and Ann Moyer.

Paul Anderson spent many hours with Bob in his den, reading the book out loud to him, short sections at a time. He enabled Bob to hear and judge his own words objectively. Without Paul's support and trustworthy advice, Bob might not have been willing to publish this work, to be a "stakeholder" as Paul called him.

Vicki Biggs was our reader, cheerleader, and guide to the publishing world. She introduced us to John Henricksson who, with his wife Julie, polished and promoted this book. His experience, encouragement, and kind advice turned our dreams into a finished manuscript.

Harvey Stower introduced our manuscript to Ron and Lyn Klug. They led us through the editing process. Patiently, gently, and with great good humor, Ron Klug and Tim Larson gave life to our words and new meaning to our journey.

ACKNOWLEDGMENTS

There is no way that we can adequately express our gratitude to these people or to the family and friends who have shown interest in our project, prodding us along with a well-timed "How's it coming?" or "When is the book due?" We can only hope that they share some of the satisfaction we feel and the conviction that one family's experience may help others who confront Alzheimer's disease.

Preface

BOB SIMPSON, 1995

My wife and I are entering, in many ways, the unmapped country of Alzheimer's disease. This will be our chart of the journey. It is in two voices. One voice presents my insights into what I feel and learn from the disease itself. I'll try to describe it as I go along.

The second voice is Anne's as the caregiver, providing her observations on what she sees happening, as well as what is happening to her, in the process. I hope our perspectives will be helpful, that we might be able to explain what people who have Alzheimer's, and those who care about them, feel and think. We also hope this book will help those who may be developing symptoms they don't understand and might fall into the category of Alzheimer's. I want to share my experience of the disease while I can.

ANNE SIMPSON, 1999

Our purpose in writing this book is twofold. Like the dual-layer underwear we use here in the winter as the base for the North Shore "layered look," the purposes are bonded.

First, we would like to demystify Alzheimer's disease. We would like to share our story and to confront the fears that for so long have kept people from talking openly about the disease. "Secrets take energy," Bob says.

We would like to lift the shroud of secrecy and ignorance that covers people who know or suspect that they may have the disease. The more we know about the early stages of Alzheimer's, the greater our chances for finding a cure. If patients are encouraged to be honest about their symptoms and caregivers are able to voice their particular concerns, then we will be better able to learn from, understand, and help one another.

Second, we want to pass on practical advice from our experience, both for patient and caregiver. Many people have told us that they don't know how to treat Alzheimer's patients, what to say or do. They don't know what the patient or the caregiver wants. Early-onset Alzheimer's is a recently recognized phenomenon. In the past, most people afflicted with the disease were not diagnosed while they were still able to express themselves articulately. Bob and I would like to use the opportunity that medical technology has provided him to address these concerns.

We feel an urgency about writing this book! It is vitally important to me to record Bob's thoughts and feelings while he is able to express them. We both assume that the reactions he has now will be similar to others that he will not be able to explain later. It will be a guide back to him when he travels into the "unmapped country" where no one can follow, a narrow path for all who love him. Bob speaks for other patients as well as for himself, and I write for other caregivers. We want to offer support and encouragement.

I kept a very detailed record of our first two years of living with Alzheimer's. It was therapy for me to write about what was happening, to objectify and describe the progression of Bob's disease and our reactions to it. The entries were very personal. I had not meant to expose them, but we realized that they might be helpful to other people.

We have condensed some entries and discarded others, but we have not softened them or cleaned them up. The first months after the diagnosis were dark and painful; it would be dishonest to pretend otherwise. The wilderness can be a dangerous, frightening place, and we did not know our way.

But we have lived with Alzheimer's for more than four years, and it is hard to remember what our life together was like before Bob had the disease. The wilderness is familiar now. We have a map of where we have been; we can see ahead to the next bend in the path. We have come this far, mumbling and complaining sometimes, wanting to return to our old life. Yet, we are stronger for the rigors of this passage, and we are learning to travel light.

We cannot determine our pace or our final destination; we cannot make straight the path. But if we trust God to guide us, we know we will continue to be nourished by the manna of unexpected blessings.

This book could not be sub-titled *Happily Ever After with Alzheimer's Disease*. No one would believe it. No one would actually choose to live with this disease! But we don't choose Alzheimer's and, at this time, there is nothing we can do to prevent it. Still, there is hope for patients and their loved ones—hope that if we are willing to face our fears, accept our fate, and help each other as best we can, we will find companionship and courage on the journey.

An important note: In many parts of this book, Bob's reflections appear in boldface type. His words are taken from conversations he had with me or from taped interviews with other people. I transcribed them verbatim, any deletions or changes being made with his approval. In most cases, Bob's remarks are clearly separate from mine. But in some cases, for clarity, our reflections are blended.

A final note: At the request of the publisher, we have changed the names of friends to protect their privacy. We hope that they and our readers will understand that this is an unfortunate but necessary legality. It in no way diminishes our deep gratitude for their acts of understanding and kindness.

AT THE BEACH

I often wonder about your mind—
how it feels for you
what it's like inside your head.

Is it like a seagull soaring away from your body
darting from one thought to another
swooping to gather someone else's crumbs?

Is it like the rocks
heavy, earth-bound, passive
collecting nourishment in small pools of water
or patches of moss,
And is it hard for you to know
that we who love you find support
and warm our backs by sitting next to you?

Is it like the waves
lap . . . lapping on the shores of consciousness?

You say the answers come
clear, distinct sometimes
and then, out of nowhere, a fog
blows in and lifts them off.
You say, "All I want to do is
think a little more . . . but it all goes away.
I'm surprised how fast it goes away."

You say it's like a wave that
rolls in high and full of promise
then starts to crest out
of rhythm
and spends itself too early.

You can't control the rhythm of your mind now.
You don't know where it will swoop or fly.
You can't sleep away the heavy weight inside your head.
You used to dream that you would
wake up in the morning
and be all well.

What do you dream now, I wonder . . .
Where in the mind fog is your beacon?

You point past the rocks
above the lake
to the clouds,
the high thin ribbons of clouds.

"Look!" you say
"Isn't that the kind of sky
you'd expect God to speak from?"

—Anne Simpson

CHAPTER ONE

MEET THE PATIENT AND CAREGIVER

Bob is a big man, six-feet tall in his drawn-up, stocking-footed prime, and still erect except for a slight stoop in his upper back. "The doctors thought I had polio as a child," he says. But his brother, who did not have polio, has the same slope to his back, and so does Bob's son, Mark. They share the same walk, too, though Mark's is more pronounced. Like a sailor on a listing ship, they firmly plant one foot in front of the other and lean slightly to the side, hunching their shoulders before shifting weight to the other foot. Bob's step is heavy on the heel and decisive. Sometimes the house will vibrate in cadence with it.

Bob was athletic as a high school student. ("No," he corrects me, "I played football—I was not athletic. Rather uncoordinated, in fact. Remember how I dance?") Well, he likes quiet sports now—especially golf, but also yard work, chopping wood, and walking. "It must be my Scottish background," he says. "I think I was born for strolling." And he was. He is strong, and he has great endurance. Almost daily we take a two or three mile walk. He—the sedentary one, the one who has never met a cookie or a piece of pie he didn't like—manages to scale the steep hill behind our house without stopping for breath. It irritates me not a little that I, who exercise and watch my diet, puff along behind.

Once, when we were on a trip to England, a British couple commented that Bob's eyebrows were very Scottish. "If you don't mind my saying," the woman said, "you look just like Robert Louis Stevenson." Bob was delighted, of course.

But he was probably less pleased when the woman's husband said that Bob's Scots-Irish ancestry produced ministers, like Bob, or hardened criminals. "Either way, you see," the man teased, "they might be alcoholics."

What I remember noticing about Bob's eyebrows from our first meeting almost thirty years ago is that they frame twinkling blue eyes. Gentle eyes that look right at you when he speaks, watching reactions and inviting you to respond. Eyes that smile. People are so comfortable with Bob that they do not seem to mind his asking the kinds of questions your mother taught you are impolite. "How old are you?" he'll ask a friend. He might question a stranger with a disability why he is in a wheelchair or what happened to her hand. "Does it hurt?" he may ask. "How do you feel?" He always listens to the answers. His concern is pastoral and contagious.

It embarrassed me at first—this habit he has of talking to strangers and asking personal questions. But I have never seen anyone turn away from him. I understand that this manner may be more acceptable in the Midwest, so sometimes I feared for his safety when we traveled, and I tried to hustle him along our itinerary.

Bob does not hustle himself. What he is doing, here and now, is what is important. He was never good at keeping schedules, though he tried. On New Year's Day, usually at halftime of the Rose Bowl game, he thumbed through the date books, wall calendars, and day planners that had been mailed or handed out to him as premiums during the holiday season, devising yet another scheme to "get organized." He was a cherished customer of stationery and office supply stores that time of year. He tried to force his mind to work like that of a list-maker, but his spirit wanted to be free.

Even in college, when he was going to school full-time and working three jobs (because he thought he didn't need a scholarship), he didn't keep a calendar. He didn't write down his schedule. His son Mark is like him that way, too.

When we gave him his first watch at age ten or so, he protested, "But now that I know how to tell time, do I have to wear it?"

When I first met Bob, his hair was thick and black and wavy. The barber said it was the coarsest hair he had ever seen. It isn't thick or black any more, but it is still coarse enough to be unruly, standing straight up when he wakes in the morning or when he pulls off his hat in wintertime. "How does it look?" he will ask me, as we prepare to enter a room full of people. I pat it down for him or hand him my comb.

Bob looks nice when he gets dressed up—Northwoods Minnesota dressed up, that is. He wears a cotton shirt, sweater, maybe a jacket for special occasions. But he prefers old flannel shirts and jeans, and he doesn't seem to notice when they need to be washed or ironed. His closets are jammed with work clothes that he might wear someday—never mind that they are too tight or out of style. "Just you wait," he said one time, refusing my offer to help him sort the closet. "Bell bottoms will come back ... then you'll be sorry!"

Bob loves hats: duck-billed seed caps, straw-brimmed golf hats, Greek fisherman's hats for "dress," fur-lined, down-filled, ear-flapped hats for winter. It takes him half a day to move his hats from his closet downstairs to the coat closet upstairs at the change of seasons. Usually, I suggest that this might be a good time to sort them out, but seldom is there an offering for the church rummage sale.

In his life, Bob has worn many hats: student, ordained minister, farmer, advocate for the arts and community organizations, son, brother, husband, father, grandfather, friend.

He was the youngest of five children—born during the depth of the Depression when his father earned $500 a month. The newest addition to the family certainly wasn't planned. "Surprise!" his siblings teased him, but their parents assured the other children that, in those days, none of them could be planned.

His two sisters and two brothers were born within five years of each other and Bob's earliest memories are of a gaggle of busy, boisterous teenagers in his family. Too young to join in, he learned to observe, to watch verbal doubles matches from his chair at the dining room table. "Every family needs a good listener," he says about himself, convinced that he developed the talent early, just to survive.

He also learned about sharing at that table. Even today, if we go to a restaurant and I ask him if he would like to split a dessert, invariably he answers, "Oh, noooo . . . You're an oldest child. Order your own dessert—oldest children always take more than their share!" (From my vantage point, I know that it is the youngest child who gets more than his just desserts.)

Bob was showered with love and attention from his siblings who, you might think from stories they tell at family reunions, spent their entire adolescence caring for their baby brother. He was also coddled by parents who, according to his stories at those same reunions, hardly ever left home. So he developed a talent many of us never acquire. Whether he wanted to or not, he learned to receive. All his life, Bob has been deeply appreciative of thoughtful deeds and gifts and invitations. He knows how to give in return—of his time, his talent, and his love.

When his first marriage ended in divorce, Bob was the custodial parent for three boys aged 13, 11, and 8. "I don't know what I would do differently," he says about raising them and about being a stepfather to my three children. "I probably should have been more strict," he reflects. I would suggest that he might have learned to cook! Les, Wayne, and Mark remember the years when their favorite meals were church pot-lucks.

Bob was the parent our children could interrupt. ("Daaaaad . . . I can't . . . I don't . . . I want . . . Puhleez. . . .") Now it is grandchildren who go to him. While I cook their meals or urge them to sit up at the table, he rocks the crying baby to sleep. "I like to talk to Bumpa," the older children say. They go into his den and watch him tinker with his pipe, fascinated that he actually uses pipe cleaners, those colorful chenille sticks that they have for craft projects at Sunday school. They go to him for quiet times away from the entertainment and activity Granny has planned. He says simply, "I enjoy them."

Bob enjoys being with most people but he needs time alone, too—big blocks of it. He needs time alone in his den to think or look out the window or to thumb through magazines. Our friend Rachel asked him what his greatest loss has been so far. Without hesitation he replied, "My eyesight. I can't read well . . . it's hard to tell time." Rachel is very compassionate. She can see his struggle. But many people who do not know Bob well cannot. They may ask, "Are you sure? He seems so healthy."

In fact, Bob is doing well. He wants to help and he wants to offer hope. It is very important to him that other patients and caregivers understand how he is feeling. "Don't make this memoir too serious!" he warns me. "But do make it helpful." If this journal of our experience with Alzheimer's disease can be enlightening, it will give him a sense of purpose.

When she heard about this book, his niece wrote, "It is so like Bob to be thinking about how he can help others." Indeed it is.

MEET THE CAREGIVER

I approach this task with much hesitation because Anne means so much to me. And I would like you to know her as I have come to know her over the past thirty years.

The first thing that attracted me to Anne was her enthusiasm and energy. She starts each day with a schedule, or more accurately schedules. She keeps a list of people that she writes to; she has a long list of people that she sends cards to for birthdays, anniversaries, encouragement, etc. She keeps up correspondence with many people.

Anne makes innumerable telephone calls, both local and long distance, some of which may last an hour or so. She is very much aware of people who are sick or hurting.

Despite the time she spends writing and calling, her greatest love is the out-of-doors. Every day she walks a couple of miles for exercise. She loves flowers and loves to plant flowers. She loves animals and is the primary caretaker of our Border Collies.

Anne has a deep appreciation of the Christian faith and received a Lay Diploma from United Seminary in New Brighton, Minnesota.

In so many ways, we are different. Anne is an extrovert. I am an introvert. Anne has a need for contacts with many people every day. I am satisfied with a few. Yet our values are very much the same. Since I have had Alzheimer's, Anne has been my primary caregiver, and I couldn't have a better one.

CHAPTER TWO

WARNING SIGNS

GHOSTS
The long grey cloud
hovers low over the lake,
a giant sea monster
whose muzzle stretches west
while its tail wraps the eastern horizon
supported by hundreds of
wobbly fog legs.

All day
from the window
I watch
cloud and fog and steam
change shape,
persistent as worries
that refuse to dissolve.

—Anne Simpson

People ask us how we knew—concerned people, our age mostly—wondering whether their own problems with memory loss are signs of normal aging or of something more serious: Alzheimer's disease, that dreaded "something serious" that we joke about for as long as we can.

There is no way for us to know when it began. Alzheimer's is a silent disease and we may have been slow to suspect, because Bob has "always been that way." He was the absent-minded professor type. The man who could go to the grocery store, forget his list (or forget to look at his list), and come home with two bags full of food he didn't plan to buy. The man who could drive past his own driveway, get lost in his own neighborhood, forget dates on his calendar, call his sons by the wrong names.

Nearly forty years ago, Bob wrote a letter to his extended family describing his experiences in his new job as pastor of the First Congregational Church, Grand Marais, Minnesota:

> There is an amazing spirit of enthusiasm among the congregation, but lots and lots of work to do, building a sound church program and at the same time getting acquainted. Right now my head feels like the inside of a lottery keg with names all jumbled up waiting for the drawing.

We used to joke about his inability to remember. One year he sent me a valentine that said, "Let me call you Sweetheart—I can't remember your name." He still has a sense of humor about his memory. Recently, when we were at a local restaurant, he went up to the woman sitting at the next table. "Hi!" he said. "When did you get back?" It wasn't the woman he thought it was, he found out later, but she had been on a trip. She never knew of the mistake, and he was very pleased with his good fortune.

Bob has always liked talking to people—friends or strangers. When we traveled he went outside the motel room to smoke his pipe, then he came in to tell me the local news of the day, or the weather predictions, or to regale me with stories of the people he had met.

When we went to town, he always stopped on the sidewalk to chat. "How are you?" he might ask someone. We would walk away from long and lively conversations, and he would say, "Who was that?" He knew each person, could associate him or her with a place or an event, and he genuinely cared for each one, but he could not remember the names. Sometimes our conversations were exercises in "fill-in-the-blank":

"I saw _____ today" (hint: goes to our church, works in the lumber yard).

"He said that _____ is in town for a visit" (hint: moved south to retire).

"Remember when we saw them in _____ ?"
The nouns go first. And names. "That door is closing behind me," says Bob. I remind him that it never was very wide open.

When we told a colleague of Bob's that he had been diagnosed with Alzheimer's, she reacted the way Dorothy Parker reputedly did when informed that Calvin Coolidge died. "How could you tell?" she asked. But she smiled a loving smile, and Bob laughed.

These qualities endeared Bob to me. His self-deprecating humor, his love of people, even his absentmindedness . . . after all, wasn't that brilliant mind of his chock full of deeply important spiritual and theological matters? So when did the personality quirks become annoying—even frightening—to us both?

It was probably about eleven years ago, when Bob was 55 years old. We had been married for 15 years. Our blended family was "launched," and we were welcoming our first grandchildren. We were living on our farm in Wisconsin, but we had sold the livestock, so we were no longer tied down to daily chores. Bob was an interim minister in the United Church of Christ.

We had thoroughly enjoyed full-time farming for the past ten years—the physical demands and the financial worries put into perspective by the birth of a healthy lamb, a bumper crop of hay that the boys helped us stack in the barn, or a dinner of fresh-picked vegetables.

But now Bob was grateful to get "turned out to pastor." I was happy working in the church again, too. Between interims, we thought we would have time and opportunity to travel and to be with our family. We could continue to live in the farmhouse that we loved, though we would divide our time between home and parish. With energy and enthusiasm we were planning the next chapter in our lives. But as the saying goes, "If you want to make God laugh, tell her your plans."

Bob was serving Plymouth Church in Eau Claire, Wisconsin, four days a week. His short-term memory was getting worse. Though he covered it well, he confused names of members in the congregation and he couldn't find his way around the city. Even after three years, I had to tell him which exit to take off the freeway. Still, there were extenuating circumstances: It was only his second interim ministry; it was in a strange city, and we were commuting 80 miles back and forth to the farm every week. (I had trouble with that too, and never could remember which refrigerator was out of oranges and which one had too many.)

Gail, a young seminary graduate, worked with Bob then. She filled in as secretary, then Christian education director, and then they shared the pastorate while she was waiting to discern a call. They worked well together, trusted each other, and gradually Bob and I came to love Gail as a daughter. Bob taught her about parish ministry; she taught us about family. She said to me once, "It's a little exasperating, isn't it? He never seems to know where he is going." I assured her it was. But that was just Bob. She began to look after his church schedule, remind him of appointments, tell him how to get there—just as I did with his social calendar. The years at Plymouth Church were happy and productive.

But I must have wondered about his memory then, even if I didn't know it until a few years later when Gail got married. She had been called as minister of the United Church of Christ in Clintonville, Wisconsin, and she asked Bob to perform the ceremony there. He was so pleased! He wanted to do it just right for her. He worried—I couldn't understand why he worried. After all, he had a lot of experience with weddings, and he always did a good job. He was prepared through long conversations with Gail and Charlie, and everything seemed (to me) to be in good order after the rehearsal.

But Bob spent the morning and most of the afternoon sequestered in our motel room the day of the 4:00 p.m.

wedding. He was working on the homily, studying again and again the order of worship, smoking his pipe, and eating snacks from the vending machine. I tried to persuade him to go for a walk with me—it was a lovely summer day—but he was too anxious to enjoy the outing.

We got to the church early so Bob could familiarize himself with the public address system and run through the service again. The ceremony began. Gail looked beautiful; she and Charlie were relaxed, responsive, and all was going well . . . Then, suddenly, Bob lost his place in the sermon. He blanked out. There was a long silence. I held my breath. Did the others notice? Did anyone but me suspect? It seemed that my heart stopped beating until he came back to himself and went on speaking. His message detoured from the original homily, but it was rational, nonetheless—meaningful and fine. Gail and Charlie were pleased with the service.

When the bridal party left the sanctuary, Bob came over to me. "I have to sit down." He was hot, his head felt clammy, and he looked gray. "Put your head between your knees," I said. He thought he would faint. Then he got pains—sharp chest pains. As quietly and as quickly as I could, I took him to the hospital.

We were there several hours. The team in the emergency room checked out his heart. Everything was "A-OK." He relaxed and the pain subsided. "It must be your hiatal hernia," the doctor said. Bob ate a small, bland meal and felt much better. We checked him out in time to dance the last dance at the wedding reception.

"Panic attack," said our doctor when Bob had the same symptoms for no apparent reason the following winter at home. He ran tests—cardiological, physiological, psychological, neurological. The results had more effect on our bankbook than on his diagnosis. No problems surfaced so, by process of elimination, our doctor told us he thought Bob had pre-senile dementia. At the time, that sentence sounded innocuous enough, especially when he added, "But I'm not sure. It could be stress; it could be mild depression."

The spell passed, our fear subsided, and life got back to normal. We had a lovely vacation in Arizona, planted and harvested our usual expansive garden, entertained children, grandchildren and friends at the farm, and Bob did another part-time ministry in La Crosse, Wisconsin. We enjoyed it there very much, but I kept wondering why Bob seemed to have so little energy. I remembered watching a television program about a man with Alzheimer's. I called the La Crosse chapter of the Alzheimer's Association and requested information. In the packet we received from the organization were the following ten warning signs of Alzheimer's:

1. Recent memory loss that affects job skills
2. Difficulty performing familiar tasks
3. Problems with language
4. Disorientation of time and place
5. Poor or decreased judgment
6. Problems with abstract thinking
7. Misplacing things
8. Changes in mood or behavior
9. Changes in personality
10. Loss of initiative

Bob read the list and exclaimed, "I don't have any of these symptoms!" Oh, how I wanted to believe him.

After two years in La Crosse, Bob left parish ministry so that he could work for the Northwest Wisconsin Association of the United Church of Christ. He worked part-time from our farmhouse as an advocate for rural churches. Without the stress of commuting, he did better.

I asked his sons when they came to visit if they noticed any changes in their father. "Nope. Not a thing," they would answer. But our Association Minister noticed. In a very loving way, he said to me one day, "Bob just doesn't seem to have the enthusiasm for this job that he used to have. Are you at all worried about him?" And a visiting friend from England noticed. She took me aside and gently asked, "Now what is the story of Bob's health, my dear?" We have a friend whose husband also has Alzheimer's. She wrote from Oregon:

> The early symptoms you and we experienced were there, alright, but perhaps because of the off-and-on appearances of the symptoms, together with the odd ability of the afflicted one to cover up, we all just kept on hoping for the best. I remember thinking during the "on times" that maybe I was just imagining the "off times." And the fact that relationships with other people seemed normal, on the surface, made me feel more than ever that maybe I had an overactive imagination. Sort of like Bob's kids not recognizing anything amiss when they talked to him. . . .

In the summer of 1993, for a variety of reasons, we made the major decision to sell our farm and to retire on the North Shore of Lake Superior. Bob had served the Congregational Church in Grand Marais, Minnesota, for five years, early in his ministry, and we visited the area every year after we were married in 1972. We loved the natural beauty of the community, its emphasis on arts and the environment, and we knew we had friends there. "I may have to change my diagnosis," said our doctor. "Bob seems bright and alert and very happy about this move!" He was.

"I can't believe I got all this packed!" he exclaimed, as we unloaded one U-Haul truck after another. I grumbled as I helped him carry box after box into the barn at our new house. His packing "it all" was not what I expected. But Bob worked hard, taping and marking and carrying all his boxes.

He helped with the planning of the move and the settling of our new household—a long and disrupting process which involved remodeling, redecorating, and repairs.

He talked to the carpenters and the painters about jobs they were hired to do and other projects that he wanted to do himself. He planned those projects with them, asked their advice. He was meticulous about what he wanted for his bookshelves, his closets, his workshop. He talked and talked about it, but he just didn't get started on the work. I couldn't understand his procrastination. Eventually, he finished some of his plans, and he did a very good job. He painted all of his bookcases; he hung pictures on our high, slanted, dark wood walls, and he arranged them artistically. Yet he dropped other projects for reasons neither of us could explain, and he asked the workmen to finish them.

When we were getting settled, I came to realize how hard it was for Bob to sort things out. He was unable to make decisions. Never had he been well organized, but these boxes he had packed went beyond clutter to chaos. One carton in his den held: his son's baptismal certificate from 1958, a title to land we bought in 1974, miscellaneous receipts, three nail clippers, an old pipe stem, and two current, unpaid bills. I was disgusted—and I was scared. I wanted to create order (to keep us out of jail, I joked), but I generated anger. "Don't act so superior!" Bob would assert. "This is my room. You can't take charge in here."

We had many arguments like this—stupid, unreasonable fights. Not the kind we had before, when we had honest differences and tried to hash them out. Now I was feeling more and more responsibility for running the household, and I did not want it all. He was retired, after all; I expected him to help me! Bob was trying harder and harder to hang on to the tasks he had always done (balance the checkbook, make household repairs, service the cars, help when the grandchildren visited . . .), but he got tired and forgetful and discouraged. I felt letdown because he didn't do a task he said he would do, and he got defensive, accusing me of attacking him—as I probably was.

We began to have conversations that were exercises in déjà vu. Every morning he asked, "What are the plans for today?" The routine went basically like this:

"We're going to the Adams' for dinner," I would tell Bob.

"What time?" he would ask.

"Six o'clock," I'd reply.

"Oh, yeah," he would say, seeming to remember.

At lunch he would ask again, "Do we have any plans for the rest of the day?"

I would answer, "We are going over to the Adams' for dinner."

"Oh, yeah. What time?"

"Six o'clock."

At five o'clock he would see me changing my clothes and ask, "Are you going somewhere?"

"*We're* going out for dinner."

"Where are we going?"

"To the Adams'!" I'd scream (or want to scream). "Remember?"

We went over the calendar together at least once a week. I made him a list of the events we had planned for each day and jobs he could do, but the same questions still came. I got angry, exasperated, felt sorry for myself. If he really loved me, I thought, he would listen. If he really cared, he could remember. We had these conversations so often that they began to seem normal, but fear joined our dialogue— fear and anger.

It seemed to me that Bob's feelings would boil over at inappropriate times. "We just don't seem close any more!" he raged at me one day in our new house. Workmen were on break in the next room. I didn't agree with him, but this was not the time or place to discuss our feelings. Bob and I have always been very close—"soul mates," as a friend once described us. But for the first time in our marriage, our perceptions of things were so different and our emotions so near the surface that we found it hard to listen to each other.

We took two of our grandsons on a grandparent-grandchild Elderhostel in the summer of 1994. Bob got jealous because I spent a few minutes one afternoon talking to a man in our group. I can't for the life of me remember what we talked about, but when Bob and I got into an argument about it, I told him he was "sick." I remember the surprise I felt when the word came out . . . and the cold relief when he responded quietly, "Do you really think I might be?"

But whether or not he thought he was sick, he didn't take care of himself. He never could "remember" that the doctor told him to lose weight, watch his cholesterol, and not eat before he went to bed. He slept a lot and, almost daily, he asked me, "Are you tired? Are you terribly tired?"

Bob was kind of the way he had always been, only more so. More disorganized, more forgetful, more deliberate and slow, more introverted. He seemed strangely reluctant to try things new or difficult. But he was still kind, loving, bright, and funny. Maybe, we told ourselves, reassured each other, maybe it's normal aging—the shedding process.

Bob's IQ was exceptionally high. In high school, he tested in the 99th percentile in math. One day, I was talking to Bob about a woman I had just met. "She's about the age of my sister," I told him. Bob asked how old that was. "Six years younger than me," I replied. I was testing him, I think. "Let's see," Bob said, "how old are you, again?" I told him I was 58. "Six years younger than 58 . . . hmmmm . . ." He got out pencil and paper to figure the sum.

We went to take the Minnesota drivers-license test after we moved from Wisconsin. There was one other man taking it at the same time, a truck driver who finished in seven minutes. I went over it carefully and checked all answers, still I finished in ten minutes. Bob worked on that test for half an hour!

"I started on the wrong page," he explained. It was painful to watch him, trying so hard to understand the questions and to do it right. He passed with a very high score, and both of us were relieved. He was still a safe driver.

Bob had always been at his best in small groups. He led many of them in the church—committees, study groups, fellowships. He was the catalyst who helped people work together, the presence that centered them. But two or three years ago, he began to feel uncomfortable, disoriented, in a group. The first time it happened we were on a Holy Week retreat at Ghost Ranch in New Mexico. He skipped one morning session because he couldn't keep up, felt he didn't belong. "I wish these nice people could have known me before," he said. "I'm not the same person now."

A woman in the group suggested we go to Mayo Clinic. "After all, you have one of the best diagnostic facilities in the country right in your back yard." Sometimes I wonder why it took us so long to follow her suggestion. But then I think, "Would any of us want to know that we have a disease for which there is no proven treatment and no cure?"

The second time he felt disoriented in a group was in St. Paul. We were at a workshop at St. Thomas College near the neighborhood where we lived when we were first married. We went out for a walk, past the house we had bought for our new family. "Do you remember that tree we planted?" I asked. It was a mountain ash that Bob had carefully chosen, now grown so tall he didn't recognize it. Nor did he recognize the restaurant where we ate supper, nor the school his boys attended. The church he had served looked familiar to him and the college campus, but not the walk by the river, not the boulevards of Summit Avenue.

So many memories, so many happy times . . . all gone. "I've lost my stories," Bob said. It would be another year before we made the trip to Rochester, but that day I think I knew. Maybe we both knew.

"Do you remember that saying we used to have in the 60s?" Bob asked. "It went something like this: a friend is someone who knows the song in your heart and sings it to you when memory fails." That day—that spring day in 1994, when the air was light and fragrant with lilacs, when my heart was too heavy to sing—I vowed I would remember Bob's song. One year later this journal began.

CHAPTER THREE

DIAGNOSIS

Rochester, Minnesota, is about 90 miles south of Minneapolis–St. Paul. We turned off the freeway from the Twin Cities and approached from the west; as we drove, the gray-white Mayo Building rose from farm fields like a 20-story sarcophagus turned on end. The image struck me: death and suffering up-ended by medical research.

That building, we found out, is only one of many medical buildings that comprise the Mayo Clinic. In the four days we spent in Rochester for Bob's evaluation, he visited most of them.

By sidewalk and subway tunnel, we walked from one to another. We sat in waiting rooms, some as big as train stations (and almost as poorly lighted), for hours. Bob's appointment folder was stuffed with envelopes from different departments in the clinic. Yet, somehow, his records arrived ahead of us for every appointment, the staff was courteous and efficient, testing was almost painless, and the billing was accurate. We were impressed. "They are very professional," Bob said.

I remember that the days were sunny and warm. Tulips and lilacs still shy in the north were brazenly blooming all around town. I remember that we had a fairly nice hotel room with a balcony where Bob could smoke his pipe. But there was a Middle Eastern restaurant near the lobby and, from 11 a.m. until closing, the halls smelled like soy sauce and peanut oil. I know that we went out for our meals, but I don't remember where or what we ate. We walked and talked a great deal—and we cried. I remember a small Episcopal church on a busy corner downtown. Its quiet courtyard welcomes the public. It was my sanctuary.

After four long days, the doctors gave the verdict that we both feared and expected: CLINICALLY PROBABLE ALZHEIMER'S DISEASE. "We can't be positive," they said. "We know from our testing that you have dementia. But Alzheimer's is only one of many forms of dementia. Patients have a unique pattern of plaques and tangles in their brains. We will put you in the category of 92 to 95 percent probability. It is the highest one we have. The only way to confirm the diagnosis is by autopsy." "I don't need to know that badly!" Bob replied. "You are in the early stages," the head neurologist told him. "And because you are young—in your sixties—we call it 'early onset.'"

Until recently, it was almost impossible to make even a tentative diagnosis of Alzheimer's. Now, thanks to medical technology, we were able to get a scientific explanation. Life as we had known it was turned on end.

My wife and I went to the Mayo Clinic in Rochester, Minnesota, so I could get a thorough physical exam—with the realization that what they would be measuring for, one of the things they would certainly be looking at, was the possibility that I had Alzheimer's.

At Mayo they have this all down, they have it timed; you have to stand up and sit down and do this and that. I can't remember all the tests. But I thought they did things very well. I felt supported. I would encourage people to go there.

It's much easier when you know it's Alzheimer's because you know something is wrong, and you spend a lot of energy and time . . . well, it's worse than that. You start kicking yourself. Why don't I have more energy? I've got all these ideas and all these things I want to do, but I really don't have the motivation to do them, and I get mad at anyone who suggests that I should. And you have a feeling that you're just not the same. You don't feel like you did before, and you get annoyed. You think it should change, but it doesn't.

The sooner I would have had the diagnosis, the easier it would have been—it would have been helpful. If I had gone to Mayo earlier, I think I would have accepted the diagnosis . . . well, maybe not . . . I would have been more anxious to go if I thought they would prove that I didn't have it.

MEMORIAL DAY

It was slow driving home from Rochester. The freeway arteries around the Twin Cities were clogged with vacationers. Families in station wagons, fishermen in four-wheel-drives, sailors (tan, young, and blond) pulling their boats. The sun was bright, the air warm, and Lake Superior was sparkling blue. Nature recklessly welcomed visitors to the North Shore for the first long weekend of the summer season.

I felt as if the people in every other vehicle on the road were celebrating life. I remember wondering: "On this holiday, does anyone remember to honor the dead?"

Bob prayed as I drove: "Help me, God. God, *help* me."

CHAPTER FOUR

The Dark Summer

We live on the edge of wilderness. State Highway 61 goes past our house. Where our driveway meets the road there are two official signs, one on either side: milepost 106 and "Moose Crossing." We are five miles or so as the crow flies from the Boundary Waters Canoe Area, and we are 106 miles from Duluth, the nearest metropolitan center. To our south is open horizon and Lake Superior.

We choose to live here. We do not like bustling crowds, lines, and noisy traffic. We would rather eat grilled lake trout than fast food. If driving two hours to the nearest Wal-Mart, medical specialist, or cinema is an inconvenience (and it can be), that is the price we are willing to pay to live in this small, eclectic community of artists and outdoor enthusiasts.

We are comforted by the rugged rocks, the woods, and wild creatures all around us, by nights so dark you can see each star, and by the cold, unruly, beautiful lake. Nature defines our role here. We enjoy and protect our environment; we give up all illusions that we have dominion over it.

But even though we may embrace the wilderness outside, we were not prepared to welcome it within. We struggled against fear and the unknown darkness of disease to reassert control—or the illusion of control—in our lives. Bob described his struggle in this poem:

A POEM
Of me there is three—
the one I am
the one you see
the one I want to be.

We knew from the beginning that we did not want to keep the diagnosis a secret. But we needed time to try it on, to shrug into the news that Mayo Clinic held out for us. We wanted to feel comfortable enough to mingle with people and talk about it.

When we got back from Rochester, we called our minister. The next Sunday, when we were not in church and without asking our permission, he announced from the pulpit that Bob had Alzheimer's disease. Gasp!

We were hurt and angry. Friends were shocked. They had a right to expect that they would hear the news from us. But, in the long run, he may have done us a favor. Right away we had to go out in public with our feelings, tell the facts as we knew them, and listen to the reactions of other people.

"I have to tell people what it is like while I still can!" Bob said. "I want people to understand this—then maybe I can help somebody else. I have so much to do! I want to do it right. I want to give things to people before I die."

Bob felt a need to get everything all worked out. There was always a sense that he was living with a deadline, but he didn't know when it was. It was like being in college and always having a paper due but not knowing your material.

One day he offered to sell, to a carpenter friend, the big pile of lumber that he had stored in the barn. It was seasoned cherry and black walnut that Bob once intended to use to make toys for the grandchildren or small pieces of furniture. It was a big, heavy pile that he had insisted on moving from the farm—over my heated protests. I helped him load and then unload it, board by board, from the U-Haul truck. It was not our finest day.

But there were dreams piled in that wood, dreams so important to Bob that he transplanted them to the North Shore. When we were in Wisconsin, he subscribed to woodworking magazines, he joined the Handyman Club, and he sat for hours in the space that would be his workshop—smoking his pipe, planning where he would put the table saw, how he would organize his tools. But while we were there, he never got his workshop set up. I couldn't understand it!

When we moved the wood into the barn at our new house, it happened again. Bob planned where and how he could set up his workshop in this new location. Scott, the carpenter, moved a partition for him and he had a corner space specially wired. But Bob never found the time to get it all in order. Three years later, there were boxes and boxes of stuff still unopened in that room. At a deep, unconscious level, he must have known that he wouldn't set up his workshop. It wasn't safe for him to use the machinery that he bought with such purpose and anticipation.

Scott was very happy to have the wood, of course. He offered half of it to Jay, who had built our cabinets and bookshelves. Within a few days, they had it all hauled away. Now two talented craftsmen, who have worked on our house and become our friends, had Bob's lumber. He was sad, but he was gratified. His dreams had been passed on. "When I make something, can I call you to come and see it?" Scott asked. "Please do!" Bob replied.

Bob wanted to sort his books. Who should have his collection on rural ministry, his theology books, his novels? Many were dated, some timeless.

"I want the right people to have the things I love," Bob asserted. "I don't want to burden the kids. They will want the house, or the money from the house, but they won't want all the things that are in it. I feel such a sense of urgency—I have to decide things!"

JUNE 14

We went to a church supper last night, a potluck before the Live Poets Society did a reading. Mary Lou, a member of the group, came to the supper straight from an audition for a part in the new production of *Picnic* at the Grand Marais

Playhouse. The director accompanied her. He wanted to recruit two women for bit parts in the play. "There are lots of people over at the church," she told him. "You'll find actors there!" So Dick went around the tables, stating to every woman in turn: "Just a small part . . . Won't take much time . . . You don't need experience . . . You'd be perfect."

We laughed. "It'll never be easier to get a part," said one woman at our table. Her husband agreed. "Today Grand Marais, tomorrow Broadway."

When he came to me, I said it would be fun, but I didn't think I'd have the time. I said I would think about it. "She's wavering!" Mary Lou teased. I said I would talk to my husband. "Well, where is he?" Dick asked. "Do it now!" I told him it would be a long talk. Trying to ignore his "you're a liberated woman" stare, I went to the back of the room where he had laid out the schedule of rehearsals. When I saw how much time the bit parts demanded, I told him no. I definitely could not be in the play. Bob did not hear our conversation.

Bob was quiet for the rest of the meal, disappeared while I helped clear the tables, went into the sanctuary for the program, and sat down without saving me a seat. I read my poems nervously, knowing he was upset but not knowing why. When it was over, we walked to the car without speaking. On the drive home, I asked what was wrong. Bob said, "I wish you hadn't brought it up. I'd almost forgotten. I enjoyed the poetry." Later, he wrote down his feelings:

I would like you to understand how I felt when I was in church, and the man came and was trying to recruit some people to be in one of the plays at the playhouse. The day before I had said I would like to have a part in one of the plays in the playhouse, but I couldn't because I wouldn't be able to remember the lines.

Being in plays in both high school and college was a great meaning-giver for me. What I feel is that I am a nobody, and I need to be seen as a person who has skills. I wish you could have said, "Bob was very active in the theater, and I would like to talk it over with him." Then I would feel like I existed and had some value.

I doubt if there is anything I can do as well as you, but I need you to help sing my song when I can't remember the words. I want to support you as much as I can. I know what I can do is very limited. I will try to do the best I can to help you, and I hope we together can support each other. I can feel it, but I can't articulate it well.

For years, Eloise [Bob's sister who has Alzheimer's] did all the cooking—and she was good. I wonder if some of her anger now is because she isn't needed for anything? John does it all.

I still want to be needed in some way. I would like you to talk things over with me, even if I can't respond well. I still need to hear "I need you." Even when I can't believe you do.

Mary Lou was right—I was wavering. I have never been in a play, I thought it would be fun to try something new, to be with people who lead more normal lives, to laugh and study and, even for a few hours a day, forget all about Alzheimer's disease. I thought Bob would enjoy coming to rehearsals. He has always loved the theater.

I did not want to act "better" than Bob. That would be ridiculous! I just wanted to have some fun, make contacts, learn new skills, and expand my horizons. I did not want the world to close in too soon.

JUNE 19

It seems to happen over and over . . . Bob and I go out together, I am feeling comfortable, enjoying the people we are with, having a good time. Then somehow, intuitively, I know that Bob is upset—probably upset with me—and I don't know why.

Last Sunday at church he was sullen because I talked to people in the narthex before we went in to worship; afterwards, I moved around to talk to others during the coffee hour. Bob stood off by himself. Gone was his usual free and easy approach to mingling with people—something he has always done specially well in a church setting.

I don't understand. We used to be so good together in a group. Laughing, teasing, feeding each other stories, listening, but now I can't tease. He thinks I am putting him down.

It's a joke, our going to church together! You always go and talk to people. I sometimes wish you could include me in the conversation. I don't belong. I never in my life felt so much like I don't belong. No one wants to talk to me.

People instinctively talk to you. It's like I'm nothing. Oh, they'll say, "Hi, Bob," but right away they start visiting with *you*, and I'll just stand there. It used to be they would talk to me, too. But I was more sure of myself then, I could take a more aggressive stance and start a conversation. Now I know I make people anxious. I'm sure I pick up more vibrations now . . . I don't seem all that different to myself, but people treat me differently when they know I have Alzheimer's.

JUNE 25

Bob and I were sorting books for the Friends of the Library sale. He has a collection of plays, paperbacks mostly—many of them going back to college days. I asked if he wanted to save them. His eyes filled with tears and he said, "I won't be reading much."

Bob, the brilliant, insatiably curious man, the voracious reader, had said this. The husband I used to criticize because he always had his nose in a book when I needed help around the house had said he wouldn't be reading much.

What is the matter with me? I feel so limited! I look right at something and I can't see it, can't make the connection.

When we remodeled this house, we put new bookcases in his den. He didn't arrange them for a long time, and I wondered why. I understand now—as I understand his secretive ordering of condensed books (preachers and writers don't approve of condensed books), and the energy he spends every day trying to digest magazine articles.

What I can't begin to fathom is the pain it must cause him to know he will have to give up reading! This disease doesn't just mean gradually losing things. It also means anticipating losses, going through long periods of mourning before the final separation. Then anticipating another . . . and another.

I have not been reading much myself lately. Is it because we spend so much time outside on these long summer days? Maybe. But I know that I feel uneasy because Bob can't read well, and I do not know how to share my pleasure in a book, or insights I glean from reading, without making him feel sad.

JUNE 27

Bob has periods of anxiety, often at night or in the early morning. They are probably a mild form of the "panic attacks" he had before the diagnosis.

Why am I so anxious? So anxious . . . I feel like I am shaking inside. I don't know why. Somehow, it always has to focus on something. Today it is the book sale . . .

I think I have always been this way to a degree. I can remember when I was sick as a child, my legs would keep running, even in bed. . . . I've got to do something physical. I like to do jobs. There's a double benefit: exercise and production. I want to do something simple. Make me go outside and get exercise! I feel so much better when I can work. If I stay inside, I just sit and feel sorry for myself.

JUNE 30

Bob was restless in the night. At about 3 a.m. I realized he was not in bed. I wandered, bleary-eyed, until I found him in his den. He was sitting in the dark. Finally, he blurted out what bothered him.

I see all the signs. I'm here but I'm not here. . . . You come into my room and turn on the lights—it's unconscious, I know. My brothers and sisters call and talk to you; they are afraid I'll forget.

When we play golf, it's like I'm invisible. No one talks to me. I'm not blaming them. I don't have much to say. I can't remember where the ball went, can't find the right club . . .

I can remember when people wanted to come to see me . . . I don't seem that different to myself, but people treat me differently now. They are not mean, not even thoughtless . . . They just think I'm not as interesting to talk to—I can't react the way I did before. I don't seem to be able to talk back as I would have once. They are probably scared, uncomfortable, the way I used to be when I started calling on patients in the hospital. I didn't know what to do.

That's just the way I see it. I don't know if anything can be changed. The world has to be like that. You have to make your own journey. You have to prepare. It's like when you graduate from high school. As seniors, you feel so secure. You have a place. I was president of the student body. Everybody "needs" you—and then you graduate.

You go back to the high school once, and that's all you can stand. Nothing has changed; everything has changed. You don't belong there any more. You have moved on to something different. I remember when I went back to a high school football game in Madison. I never did that again. I remember the terrible loss I felt forty years later when the school itself closed down.

In order to move onto the next step, there has to be something you are moving to. You go off to college—everything is new. You do that many times in life. Life is a series of journeys. You always have to get kicked out. There is a series of adventures you need to go through—life pushes you there. You may try to hold on but the system moves you on, even if you are not ready. You've had your time. . . .

JULY 6

Bob tried again and again to read about his disease. As best he could, he wanted to learn. He was especially concerned about how much time he would have. We had a conversation early this morning:

"I guess I shouldn't have read all that Alzheimer's literature," Bob said. "I didn't sleep . . . a terrible night. I was so anxious, I almost woke you. I'm glad I didn't. It will only get worse. After awhile it will be worse for you than for me . . ."

"No it won't."

"Will you be okay?" he asked.

"I'll be lonely."

"I hope it doesn't go on too long," Bob said quietly.

"I do! I hope it is slow and gradual."

"Do you have friends here?" he asked.

"Yes, good friends. I will need professional advice and support, too. I'm sure I can get them here. Somehow."

"I'm so sorry," Bob responded.

"*I'm* so sorry!"

JULY 14

One of the hardest things for me to accept is the emotional outbursts. Bob has always been so gentle, even-tempered. He would get angry, of course (so would I), but before this disease, we could talk it out. It might take time. We decided early in our marriage not to go to bed with a quarrel—and, indeed, there were some sleepless nights.

But this summer it seems the outbursts come from nowhere, and I don't know how to react to them. It is hard for me to control my emotional response. I am defensive and hurt, but I can't fight back because it isn't fair to Bob. Yet I need to express my feelings, or at least identify them, so they will not block our communication.

Sometimes Bob is justifiably angry. Other times I am the one who is handy. I try to accept the feelings he projects onto me because I understand what he is doing. Whether I want to admit it or not, I do the same to him.

Unfortunately, it is easy for me to blame myself when Bob is angry. For his sake as well as my own, I know I need to untangle my feelings from his.

I am taking over more and more of his jobs. I don't want to do it and he doesn't want to let them go, so many of the outbursts are about power and control. I know that I step on Bob's toes a lot as I stumble around trying to be Super Wife and Super Caregiver. I also know that I feel overwhelmed by the new responsibilities and by fear of a future that seems dark and murky. This is not the radiant serene sixties we had imagined. As our brother-in-law says, "The golden years have some tarnish on them."

Bob's feelings do not seem abnormal, just exaggerated and sometimes inappropriate. I can blame them on his disease, but if I do that I diminish him and his emotions as well. (I also avoid my own responsibility for provoking them.) On the other hand, if I treat the outbursts as appropriate even when I think they are not, if I try to draw out Bob's feelings and talk about them, sometimes we can get to the issue behind the issue. It takes time! I need to learn not to resent the time.

I need to learn, too, that there is more than one way to reach resolution. The straight-ahead, up-front approach that is my specialty doesn't work now. Every problem is not a nail; I need more tools than a hammer. As the literature says, no one ever won an argument with an Alzheimer's patient. I don't want to argue anyway—though I do it. What I really want to do is to understand.

Emotional outbursts are common, understandable. This is a hard way to go. You have the ideas, but the words don't come out. You see the words, but you can't read them. You

can't communicate! It hurts. More than anger, I feel hurt. I know a lot of patients get angry. I understand why.

JULY 16

I'm lonely. I just want to be with you. I'm jealous of the time you spend with others. We don't have that much time left.

JULY 20

It isn't fair! My hands are sore and swollen from arthritis—I suppose from hauling rocks yesterday . . . My knee is stiff . . . Now my hemorrhoids are bleeding! I'm falling apart. Doesn't it seem bad enough that a person has to get Alzheimer's without having hemorrhoids?!

JULY 26

Don't ask me—tell me! Then I don't feel pressure. If someone says, "Do you remember. . . ?" or "Do you know who I am?" the pressure makes me panic. It's like a child trying to say the right word, getting frustrated because grown-ups don't understand. I want people to be as patient with me as they are with children.

It helps so much when people tell me things—tell my story . . . things I've seen or done or what I've meant to them. It's like I still exist. I'm the same person I've always been, only I can't express myself so I get angry—only I'm not really angry, I'm frustrated. If I can reduce the anxiety, I can last longer. I used to blame myself, try harder to keep up. Now I know to retreat.

AUGUST 1

Our contacts at the Alzheimer's Association have urged us to join a support group. The Mayo Clinic nurses thought Bob should participate in one for patients in the early stages. They told me I should join one for caregivers of Alzheimer's patients. Geographically, our county is the largest in the state. But the year-round population is 4000. Such groups do not exist here. "Well, start one!" they said. "Couldn't you drive to Duluth?"

There are lots of reasons why I would not want to make the 100-mile trip every other week. There are very few advantages to having a group long-distance. But the real reason I hesitate to join a group is that I do not want to be with people who are farther along the path than we are. And Bob does not want to join a group of other diseased people. He already feels isolated. He would rather be surrounded by healthy people who affirm and include him than be segregated with Alzheimer's patients.

This summer we were put in touch with another clergy couple through the Mayo Clinic. Luther and Kris were visiting Duluth and they drove up the shore to join us for lunch. They are lovely people, about our age. He was diagnosed with Alzheimer's just two years ago, at the age of 59. He is still ambulatory, and he can make himself understood in conversation, but he has great difficulty eating. He cannot go to the bathroom by himself, and he is extremely dependent on his wife. His disease has progressed very rapidly! "That's what happens when you get it young," Kris told us. She tried to be gentle. "I urge you to join a support group."

The couple lives in Minneapolis where there is adult day care for him, support groups for both patient and caregiver, a large chapter of the Alzheimer's Association and many resources available to them through other community organizations. They moved to Minnesota from New York after the diagnosis to be near their son's family. They are newcomers to the Twin Cities, so these support systems have been a godsend. I am very happy that they exist for them.

But for me, at this time, I do not want them. I do not want to schedule emotional outbursts for the first and third Mondays between 2:00 and 3:30 p.m.! I do not want to surround myself with people who are in pain as great as my own (or greater), nor to concentrate my energy on loss and grief.

I feel, as Bob does, that reading materials, looking too far ahead, and being with other patients can be as depressing as it is helpful. We need to plan ahead, of course. But we could become so paralyzed by fear of the future that we don't enjoy the present. I have talked to staff at the nursing home, the hospital, the clinic, and the public health nurse about our needs now and those anticipated for the future. We know what resources are available but we can't know what we will need or when.

So, for the time being, we want to be surrounded by healthy people. Maybe that isn't realistic. But sometimes our life seems so normal and Bob so much the same as ever, we don't want to think too much about the future. It is a relief to be open about our problems, but sometimes we just want to ignore them. Is that neurotic?

Our close neighbor, whose mother has Alzheimer's, is in the general Caregivers support group that meets in Grand Marais. She says that when people ask caregivers about the patient, most of them began their answers with "I. . . ."

When I get to that point, I told her, when I can no longer separate Bob's health from my own, then I would like to join the group. Someday, I know I will need it and be grateful for it. She promised to tell me when she thinks the time has come.

In the meantime, I feel guilty for not having more contact with Kris and Luther. We write letters and talk on the phone occasionally, but we have not been to visit them. I know he is deteriorating quickly and perhaps I want to avoid him for the same reason people avoid us. Anyone can get Alzheimer's—no one wants to be confronted by the ravages of it. Many caregivers are isolated because friends "can't bear" to see the patient's condition. It was difficult for both Bob and me to be with his sister after he was diagnosed with her disease, but we have been gratified to find the spirit of Eloise still alive inside her shriveling mind and body.

To everything a season . . . a time to live and a time to die. A time to celebrate health and a time to acknowledge disease. But we wonder if we can do both at the same time—that is the question.

AUGUST 4-8

Gail was here! This busy young minister who has been both colleague and "daughter" to us for the past ten years took five days off to visit the North Shore for the first time.

"It was so wonderful to have her here!" Bob exclaimed after she left. "She treated me just the way she always did—like a real person."

Gail and I took a poetry-writing class at the Art Colony. We read and wrote and worked together from 9 a.m. to 3:00 p.m. She had time to be with Bob in the afternoons and evening, while I plugged away at the word processor, producing drivel. Then she would get up early in the morning, sit in the armchair in the living room, bask in the eastern sun—feet on the ottoman, notebook and pencil in hand, a cup of tea on the table by her elbow. In less than an hour, she composed one gem after another to read in class.

Her talent is the only thing that I could hate her for. Otherwise, her presence here brought unmitigated joy. "Oh, good!" she said when she came into our house for the first time. "It smells just like your old house."

One morning, as we drove to class, Gail asked me, "Why isn't Bob reading?" She missed the conversations they used to have about new theological writings and church studies or even novels they enjoyed.

"He can't." I explained the vision problems Bob was having. She sat stunned and silent until we arrived at class. Getting out of the car she said quietly, "I guess I can't know what it is like for you. . . ."

She said that again when she witnessed a scene at the house. The plumber was there to fix a broken faucet. I went down to Bob's den to get a check for him from our old farm account—the one we use for capital improvements. Bob grabbed the check out of my hand.

"I'll do it!" Bob asserted. "You keep saying to the plumber, 'I . . . I want you to change the pipes . . . I have checked the faucet.' You can't do everything! I'll pay the bill."

The plumber waited . . . I waited . . . Gail went to her room. It was a long time before Bob came back. He brought the plumber cash. "Oh," said the plumber. "This is different! I don't usually get money."

Later, after he had left, Gail found me crying. I told her that I had provoked Bob by being efficient and taking over in an area that used to be his. I knew that he was only partly blaming me. He felt frustrated, angry with himself, useless.

"But why is anyone to blame?" she asked. "Is it better for him to blame you than himself?"

I said yes before I really thought out the answer. Yes, because I am healthy and Bob is not. Later he reflected on his frustration: "I couldn't write the check. I'm sorry. I guess it is a pride thing. That was my checkbook. I always had it balanced. I always knew exactly how much money was in there. I tried to write him the check, but I couldn't remember his name. I know he told me, maybe two or three times, but I couldn't remember."

After this incident, Bob gave up the checkbook.

There were a few shadows. But mostly Gail's visit was bright sunlight. We laughed, ate many good meals, took walks, played with the dogs, and sat by the lake. We talked about her church, her farm, and the life she shares with Charlie. She is so happy in her marriage and in her church work that we rejoiced with and for her. "You did a good job," she said to Bob, her mentor in the first church she served and the officiating minister at her wedding.

I told her that Bob would be sending her his books on rural ministry when he was ready to part with them. She understood the importance of the gift and wrote him later:

THANK YOU NOTE
I used to love to wear
my sister's clothes—
the wispy Indian cottons,
tiny violet prints
straw hats, but mostly,
the scent of her on everything, spicy and grown-up.
Sometimes when she was away
I would open her closet door
and bury my nose
in the ruffles breathing deeply. . . .
Like when I unwrapped
the box of your books
which arrived by mail in winter—
the titles, interesting enough, but more than that
the aroma of your library
wafting upward from the carton:
tobacco smoke, wood and autumn
and the scent of your fingertips
where you have stroked the pages searching for
    something.
I longed to close the box tightly
to preserve the essence inside
but thought instead, with abandon,
to leave it open
to set the little spirit free
to let it dissipate
the way love leaves a house
never quite empty.
                —Gail Irwin

AUGUST 8

It takes so long . . . for nothing! Things I could do in first grade—set my watch, write numbers . . . it's so much work! I wonder why it is . . . if we talk about money, for instance, I can follow the discussion and understand the concepts. I can make change. But writing checks?! I can't do it! I'm exhausted. I don't mind that it takes me so long, really—I just mind that I don't know how any more. Things that I did all the time . . . Now nothing is familiar. I can't figure it out the way I used to, can't push myself to get things done. Why is that? It's so frustrating!

AUGUST 12

Bob's oldest son, Les, came from New York to visit during Fisherman's Picnic. On Saturday we were at the beach. We ordered iced lattés from the outdoor cart and relaxed after strolling through town, talking to tourists and residents, shopping at the booths set up for the gala weekend celebration in Grand Marais.

I walked down the beach to talk to a man who had an English springer pup on a leash. Bob got up, came over and said something to me, which I didn't quite catch, then he turned and walked to the Trading Post with Les. I finished my latté, browsed the tables and sales racks outside the Post, then went inside.

Bob was upset. I didn't know why. He was very angry when we got home, sullen and weeping all evening. He tried to explain it but he couldn't. "Don't you suppose he's frustrated?" Les asked.

We spent a very quiet evening—not what we had planned, with all the festivities in town. I did some cooking; Les read in the living room, close to Bob's den but not intruding on his father's privacy.

Sunday, Bob was still upset. He told me, finally, that it was because he was convinced I wanted to stay with that man. For heaven's sake! I would have gone up to a woman or a child—to anyone who was with that springer. I love puppies and someday, when our border collies are gone, I would like to have a small house dog. I wanted to cuddle the pup and to ask about the breed.

I was not aware how Bob was feeling; I didn't know he wanted to leave the beach and the Fisherman's Picnic crowds. I didn't pay enough attention to where he and Les were going. I was guilty of being selfish, rude, insensitive, slow. But guilty of wanting to stay with that man—no. A few days later we talked about it.

It's my memory that I told you I wanted to go. You said it would be just a minute, but you stayed and talked to that man. I went in to the Trading Post with Les, came out to find you, and you ignored me. You were still talking!

I wasn't jealous. I was lost . . . so lost. I felt like you would talk to anyone else but me.

You are so nice and friendly to other people, and you just ignore me. You want to be with "real people." You are staying away from me. Already you know that I will be a burden.

I was just wearing out. I couldn't understand why we didn't go home. You seemed to have no sense of what I was feeling. I was trying so hard to keep going, but the day had just gone on too long. All my wires started crossing.

It was like being in molasses. . . . More and more people, more talking, and I was just stuck there. You were driving— I couldn't leave without you.

I wanted to cry.

Bob misread my motives, but I had let him down. I tried to reassure him that I would be there for him, that I would support him, care for him, and stay with him for the rest of his life or mine. But I wanted to cry, too, because I didn't know if I could do it well. I wanted to cry because I saw him losing confidence in himself. And I wanted to cry for myself because I knew I was losing, too—losing the dream of growing old with my husband, my lover, companion, and closest friend.

I wanted to cry because maybe he was right. Maybe I was protecting myself, "doing my own thing," instead of working with him to adjust to this disease together. I have read that when people are diagnosed with Alzheimer's disease, family and friends come close, then start to pull away.

Looking back on this weekend, both of us can see how confused our emotions were, how they were bruised in bumping against each other. It seems more simple now.

I would just tell you that I have to go. Now I can be straight. Back then, I didn't know how to handle it. I couldn't name my feelings.

People have to understand about Alzheimer's patients. We're still here. We still have ideas and can express them. Just be patient and listen to us. We are real people! There is a difference between the people and the disease. The disease is what makes us different.

AUGUST 20

Bob and I have always juggled *chronos*, calendar time, and *kairos*, meaningful time. He would say that I am overly scheduled. I would say that he is "chronologically challenged." Bob procrastinates and makes decisions at the last minute, depending on how he feels. I like to have things decided—dates filled in, work assigned—well ahead of time.

Often, when we get together now to talk about our plans, I say too much, give him too many choices, and he balks.

But I don't want to make plans without Bob's input. I don't know how much activity he can tolerate. Can he go out alone? Can I? How often and how long?

August is bustling with its annual infusion of tourists, houseguests, and summer activities. We have a lawn to mow and flowers to tend and many other outdoor projects. A long "to do" list for a short summer. There are also invitations to local events and family gatherings across the state.

I can't make decisions. I'm a failure. Anybody could do this! Maybe I can't talk about the calendar any more—it gives me a headache.

But I like having ordered projects to do . . . so they don't tumble down on me. It's hard when I have two things. I get overwhelmed . . . I used to be able to let things pile up and not get overly anxious. Now I'm like a donkey between two bales of hay. I get confused. My mind goes blank. I stay and starve in the middle.

AUGUST 28

There is no medically proven treatment for Alzheimer's disease. There is no cure. But there are drugs that are being used experimentally to control the symptoms. Bob has been strongly encouraged by the Mayo Clinic to try one for their research program. He wants to cooperate not only for himself, but also because he might contribute to a body of knowledge that will help others, maybe his own family.

The doctors at Mayo strongly recommended a drug. I had to take four pills a day, had to have my blood tested every week. I did that for about a month but I kept feeling worse and worse. Still, there were good times in between so I couldn't tell if it was the pills.

I felt "spacey," couldn't track . . . I didn't feel good about it. I didn't feel I could do jobs myself. I felt almost tranquilized, felt more dependent. I took all those pills. I wish they had a "happy pill!" It got to be too much, so I quit—but not for long. I started again, because the doctors urged me to.

After six weeks, the doctor doubled the dose. Two pills for breakfast. I just sat there . . . shaking all over . . . never could stop. We called the nurse. She talked to the doctor and then called back with an answer: "Drug overdose." It cleared up after awhile, and I stopped taking the drug.

Within four or five days I was feeling better than I had in some time.

I feel much better now. I have some of the same feelings but not all the time. I take rest spots; sometimes I sleep, and then I'm clear again for awhile. I'm sure other people have different reactions. Now all I take are vitamins. I'm strong and my health is basically good.

CHAPTER FIVE

Autumn Changes

My father died when I was 22. I was twelve years younger than Bob's youngest son is now. I came across a picture of Dad the other day, and all the emotions that initially flooded me forty years ago washed through my heart again.

I understood, in a bright instant of knowing, why I get impatient, even angry, with Bob's "boys." I understood why I sometimes want to shake them by the scruffs of their thirty-something necks and say, "Look! . . . Listen! . . . Attention must be paid!"

I never said good-bye to my father, who died suddenly and unexpectedly of a massive heart attack. He passed away less than an hour after leaving his doctor's office with a clean bill of health. He was 50 years old.

I never said "thank you" or "I'm sorry" or "I love you" or "God bless . . ." All those things left unsaid spill over into tears, even now, when I see his picture. I didn't have time or opportunity to reach closure with my father.

Many other ties to family and friends were sundered by divorce, so all the loose ends in my own life make me want to help, urge, cajole Les and Wayne and Mark to tie everything together.

Our friend Dave lost his mother to Alzheimer's after she had lingered for many years with the disease. He was a loving and attentive son, yet he still worries about what he could or should have done during his mother's final days. He said to me, "Someday Bob won't know you. How then will you say good-bye?"

I couldn't answer his question except to say that it is the present that concerns me, not the future. Like Dave, I'm sure that all of us will have some regrets. But If we do for Bob and with him whatever we can now, then, at the end, I hope we will be able to let him go. We have the blessing—and the curse—of watching Bob deteriorate and sharing the experience with him. That's why Alzheimer's is called "the long good-bye."

Bob's sons have special, sacred time right now when he is alert and strong, responsive to them, able to both give and receive support. I wish they could see how lucky they are! I wish they would hallow this time. But it is not fair for me to project my own regrets onto the children.

It has been very hard for them to accept their father's illness. For three years before we went to the Mayo Clinic, I shared my concerns with them. I described the symptoms I observed; they dismissed and comforted me. "He's always been kinda spacey, you know," they would say.

"Does Wayne see what is happening to his father?" I blurted once to my daughter-in-law. Lori thought for a moment, then answered for her husband: "No . . . He has always been Wayne's hero." I wonder what signs I refused to see of my own father's illness.

All of Bob's sons were stunned by his diagnosis of Alzheimer's disease. They turned to him in their frustration, for support: "Call Mom," said Wayne. "She's very upset." "Call Mark," said Les, "he's very upset." Mark said, "I think I need counseling. Will you pay?"

Bob has been the comforter, nurturer, cheerleader and supporter of his family. He holds on still, as tightly as he can, to that position. For years, his sons have called for advice, guidance, emotional support and, yes, financial assistance. They are self-reliant now, yet Bob feels that the relationship to his sons is almost the same as it has always been. None of them want it to change: "Be Dad, Dad!" Bob is afraid of letting them down with this disease: "They sound so relieved when I tell them I'm okay. They are good kids and they've had a rough time . . . I'm still their father, after all. The only one they have."

Of course he's their father—he always will be! But change is inevitable. All of us know it . . . and we don't want to know.

The first time Les came for a visit after the diagnosis, he brought a scrapbook of his work in New York—pictures of the talk show he hosts on cable TV, reviews of the play he wrote and produced. It earned him an arts grant. When we went to see Wayne in Wisconsin, he took Bob on a private tour of the canning factory where he is supervisor. We stopped to see Mark on our way home from the Mayo Clinic; he took Bob to his radio station, introduced him around the small Iowa town.

Bob is proud of his sons; he asks nothing of them except that they take good care of themselves and the next generation. But my expectations of Bob's children and grandchildren have been high . . . and unrealistic. I thought they would all understand that Bob needs to receive now, as well as to give. But how could they? They have not yet been affected much by death (thank God!), and they are too young to have seen contemporaries thrust into the caregiving role. I must remind myself that changing roles is a long, organic process. Perhaps, in time, we are able to parent our parents. But it is a new order of things, it seems unnatural— so first, the cocoon.

We all know grown children, who are by all appearances responsible, robust, and hale, who languish on visits to their parents' homes. They are unable to find the kitchen when they are hungry, to see hooks in the bathroom for hanging wet towels, to come up with their own gas money. As our wise friend Cathy says, "It's hard to give up being a kid."

We have a neighbor in her late sixties who visits her mother in the nursing home every day. She can still be moved to tears by the old woman's erratic behavior. "I want her to be the way she was!" she exclaimed to me once. Walter Wangerin Jr. explains this often painful sentiment in the following passage from *Mourning into Dancing*:

> When elders slip toward senility and children must assume the role of parent to their parents, no one should be shocked by feelings of a sudden and tremendous sorrow. Nor by feelings (oddly) of anger or depression thereafter. Even though the elder is physically present to be honored and nursed, the old relationship (that of adult to respected adult) has cracked and mended. This is, though without corpses, a death. Sorrow, anger, depression are grief, right and natural and good. (90)

A colleague in ministry tells us that he stood by his father's grave when he was in his fifties, crying, "No—not yet! I'm not ready!" Bob's sons aren't ready. Bob is not "ready" either—nor am I. We can't look at our losses head-on, but we can, and we all do, catch glimpses of them.

On his last visit, Mark sat with Bob in the den, crying. "Who will hold the family together when you are gone?" Firmly, Bob told him. "You will. You and your brothers will."

Les' work in communications and theater keeps him in New York City. Wayne needs all the time he can spare from work to be with Lori and their blended family of seven children. Mark's task is to establish himself in career and community; he would like to get married someday. Each of Bob's sons has challenges to meet and contributions to make. They are busy young men. They are like pieces of a puzzle, their lives touching only in spots, but they fit jaggedly together to form a family.

Their care and concern for Bob is obvious. If we needed help, they would come. But we will try not to make many demands on them as long as I am alive, healthy, and strong. What Bob does want, what I want for all of them, is connection: visits, phone calls, cards and photographs. Slowly, his sons are beginning to understand. If I get impatient because they seem to take him for granted, Bob reminds me that parents are in a unique position. It's hard for their children to see them as "people."

Bob's sister has Alzheimer's disease. After Bob was diagnosed, we received a letter from his niece. It honestly described experiences of adjusting to her mother's illness:

> It is difficult, as a child, to stop asking how the parent's affliction will change my life and consider how it is affecting the parent's life.
>
> Very early on in my mother's disease I was visiting, and my father was out of the house. Mom got up from her nap and had no idea who I was. I told her, but she insisted that "her Mary" had blond hair (the color changed when I was about eight). Then, thinking how I would feel if I found a stranger in the house, I asked if she was frightened. She said that she wasn't and after about two hours she gradually recalled who I was. The incident made me accept the fact that she had a problem, and I was better able to understand some of what she and Dad were experiencing. For many years my sister ignored the problem, saying that Mom just had "little lapses" due to aging and Parkinson's Disease.
>
> Another facet to the child's problem is that if I admit my parent has a problem . . . then maybe that will require me to visit more, help out in some way, or take on responsibilities for which I don't feel ready. So, if I can convince myself that there is no problem, then I don't have to deal with these frightening changes or decisions—or even feelings of guilt.

Les, Wayne, Mark, and I will learn to deal with change and decision one way or another. I hope none of us will be burdened by guilt. We all are on the same journey with a man we love, though we travel different paths. We each must move at our own pace.

I ask Bob, "Do you think you will ever reach closure with the boys? Say all the things that need to be said and heard?"

"Probably not," he replied, "but maybe they will remember me laughing."

I look again at the picture of my father. I remember laughter; my heart smiles.

SEPTEMBER 26

"Don't slow your step to Bob's," people tell me. It is good advice and well-meaning, and I understand that they are encouraging me to take care of myself. But it is impossible to follow. How can I not be slowed?

Our conversations are deliberate and repetitive, our physical exercise moderate, our social contacts limited by his tolerance for outside stimulation. Bob cannot be left alone for a prolonged period of time without getting anxious, and I am as uneasy as a mother with young children about being away from the house for too long. My enthusiasm for outside activities and events has dwindled to fit the time and energy I have left to be involved in them.

I am more tied down to household chores. Again and again, there is friction when I step into Bob's territory to do (reluctantly) jobs that have traditionally been his. Day after day, he relinquishes control over his life and, unwilling, I assume it. We squabble more now. Yet, in many ways we are closer than ever.

I prepare for a future that will not include him; at the same time, I try to be present to my husband—still vibrant and alert, still loving and gentle. And he, dependent on me and resenting it, wants to be needed still.

I do need him—my beloved companion, my teacher, my confidant and friend. I need the one with whom I share dreams and debate ideas, laugh and cry, in whose presence I'm at home. Being with Bob is my greatest pleasure now, as for years it has been. But where once we had minutes together, we now have (and need to have) long hours.

I am sixty! In this one year I have shifted, with a grinding and stripping of gears, from an active mid-life into a quiet old age. It seems that when we are young our energies are channeled by social conventions, outside authority, or the number of hours in a day. When we grow older, we are limited from inside by our own diminishment.

I had imagined my sixties as an active time, a time when Bob and I would still be alert and energetic; retirement would give us free time to be engaged in the lives of our grandchildren, in the church and community affairs. Bob and I planned to travel, explore new places, develop new skills . . . He wanted to be a bogey golfer, and I was determined to enter the 21st century computer literate. We would have family reunions and quiet days with old friends. I wanted to do more writing (not a journal on Alzheimer's disease, but volumes of magnificent poetry or the great American novel).

I looked forward to my sixtieth birthday as much as I had dreaded my fiftieth. When I passed fifty, I had outlived my father and all of my grandparents. At that time I did not want a party; I felt more like having a wake. I spent the day crying. Bob asked, "Couldn't I even take you out for dinner?" I wouldn't let him.

But as my sixtieth birthday approached, I was so surprised and grateful to be healthy that I wanted a dance. I talked about a reunion of high school classmates to celebrate the milestone together. I dreamed about a trip to Britain, the land of my ancestors.

As the milestone grew near, I realized I would not enter my sixties with joy. I felt betrayed. So did Bob.

"This should be a big deal for you!" he said. "I want to plan a surprise party, but I don't know how. I'd like to invite some of your school friends to visit, but how do I find their names? Let's have a BIG celebration! I want to get it all done . . . I used to do such clever things."

We didn't have a party but, as it turned out, my birthday was lovely. Bob and I went to Duluth for two days, stayed in a fancy room at Fitger's Inn, walked by the lake, went out for lunch with a very special friend, and enjoyed the most glorious autumn weather that the North Shore has to offer. The morning we left for Duluth, Bob went into town early. He came back with an enormous hand-woven basket brimming with flowers. "Count the blossoms," the card read. There were sixty! Red and yellow and pink and purple and green and white—gaudy, garish, spectacular!

"I planned it all!" Bob exclaimed.

"But what will we do with them?" I asked.

"Take them, of course!"

We covered the basket loosely, carefully and "take them" we did. We took them to Fitger's. Then we took them all the way to Madison, Minnesota, Bob's hometown, where his siblings gathered to say good-bye to Eloise, their oldest sister. It was a bittersweet day with a family I love, a quiet celebration. More simple, surely, than the ones I had planned. And deeper.

I wouldn't have chosen it, of course; I would not have wished to spend my birthday marking death as well as life, but there was no choice. Sometimes we can tailor our environment to fit our needs. Other times, perhaps most times, we must make the alterations in ourselves. So I changed my expectations and slipped into a day that befit the occasion, just as a slower life at sixty must fit me now.

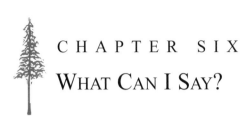

CHAPTER SIX

What Can I Say?

In *Reaching Out*, Henri Nouwen discusses the gift of helping others in pain:

> Those who do not run away from our pains but touch
> them with compassion bring healing and new strength.
> The paradox, indeed, is that the beginning of healing is
> in the solidarity with the pain. (61)

Reflecting on Nouwen's words, I am haunted by a conversation I overheard yesterday in the grocery store. The checkout girl was telling a customer about her father-in-law:

"We'll be gone for Thanksgiving, you know. Gotta go to California to visit my father-in-law. He has Alzheimer's, so we'll probably put him in a home.

"It won't be a happy trip. He's getting difficult. He stays home alone all day, and that's not good for him. They just took away his driver's license. He gets lost if he goes out the back door.

"He brought it on himself, though. He used to be such a great gardener, put in all these plants and flowers and trees. Now he doesn't even take care of them! If he would have just stayed active, this woulda never happened.

"He came to stay with us this summer—three months, very difficult. One night we called him for supper, but he went into the bedroom. Came out awhile later and got mad at us because we hadn't included him in the meal. 'Why didn't you tell me you were eating?' he asked. Well! We had told him—he was just being difficult!"

"How old is he?" the customer asked.

"Sixty-six. It does seem awfully young to put him away. Me? I'm going to stay busy and active till I drop. It'll never happen to me!"

This kind of misunderstanding seems to be everywhere. Bob and I went to a new barbershop and, after Bob had his hair cut, I explained that I would pay the bill for both of us because he had Alzheimer's. "Oh, that's too bad!" the barber said. "He must have been a wonderful man . . . er . . . I guess he still is wonderful."

We were having lunch in town. A woman we have known for a long time came over to our table. She had just opened her mail and received news that a friend of hers had died of Alzheimer's. "Well, it's all for the best," she said. "She came to visit last year, and it was too difficult for me. I just couldn't handle her. So much cooking, and she was a fussy eater. . . ." When she left, Bob commented, "There ought to be a law! What to say—or not to say—to make an Alzheimer's patient feel worthwhile."

We decided to jot down what has been helpful in our experience, because when someone has a loss, of any kind, we all wonder what to say. And many times we are not sure that we will say the "right" thing, so we say nothing at all.

Our suggestion, first of all, is say *something*. Say, "I'm sorry"; say, "I'm thinking of you"; say, "You are in our prayers"; or say, "How are you doing?" If it is said with love and concern, the words don't matter. If you feel that you might blubber, don't worry. When you express your emotions about our loss, we know that you are trying to understand our feelings and that you are willing to share them.

Talk to us in person. Come to visit, go out of your way to start a conversation in the grocery store, on the sidewalk in town, at church, at a friend's house—wherever we may run into one another. If you say nothing when we meet, we will think you do not care. We all know it's true that the opposite of love is not hate, but indifference. If you are silent, we will feel that you are indifferent to the cataclysmic thing that is happening in our lives. You may not mean to give that impression, and we may even know that, but nonetheless we will feel let down.

When my father died, almost forty years ago, my mother was offended if people mentioned his death in public. It was considered to be "poor taste" at that time because it might upset the person in mourning (who, evidently, was supposed to be as stoic and impassive as Jackie Kennedy at her husband's state funeral). But I felt that people who ignored the most important thing that had ever happened to me— my father's death—were indifferent to, or unwilling to accept, the hurt and very vulnerable young person that I was and that I had a right to be.

If you cannot talk to us in person, use the telephone. Write a note. This year, in our Christmas card, we told long-distance friends that Bob had been diagnosed with Alzheimer's disease. Some people didn't respond to the news at all. (Were they afraid of saying the wrong thing? Were they unwilling to face their own fear of getting this dread disease . . . or even of getting older?)

Others tried to pass off the bad news and quickly move on to something more cheerful: "Don't worry, the doctors can give him something . . ." "We are fine and healthy in our family, too bad about you . . ." "Life's weird . . ."

But the most helpful responses we received simply acknowledged what we had said: "We are devastated"; "How sad"; or "You are much too young!" We felt heard.

We also felt affirmed by messages of hope: "These could be the best years of your life together . . ." "Sorry to hear about the Alzheimer's, but I know you can cope . . ."

It is very important to share hope and good news with Alzheimer's patients and their loved ones. In his Christmas card, one friend told us that his mother's most appealing traits came forward clearly even as her mental powers waned with Alzheimer's. Another man wrote about the very gradual decline of his father, "There can be many good years still. . . ."

Send us articles you read about new treatments, drugs, or research. Send us jokes or cartoons. Tell us the news of your family. Share any interest or activity that you can. One of Bob's highest accolades was from a golfing friend who called to tell me, "I like to play with him. He's funny!"

With Alzheimer's disease there is progressive loss, and grief is chronic. It will not go away or be cured in a month, a year . . . "It's time for you to be over it now" is a message people often give unwittingly. We will never be "over it" but we will learn, with help from friends and family and professional health care providers, to get through it. Meanwhile, stay in touch with us.

Several people told Bob how important he has been in their lives. His past was defined by what they said and his future as well. A young woman Bob has known for more than thirty years wrote:

> No matter what happens, or how you are able to respond to me, I will be there for you. I am reminded of times I shared with you years ago, when I was just a kid in the youth program at church. There are immeasurable ways in which your gentle, guiding spirit touched my life. Those tools of enrichment remain with me to this day, and I am so very grateful to you for helping to pass them on to me. Thank you, Bob. Thank you for the innumerable others you helped, too.

A friend in Amery called and said, "I will treat you as I always have." Thank you. Bob is the same person he always was! A seminary classmate wrote:

> Now that I am almost 65, I can say what I feel! I want you to know how much I value our friendship. I want you to know how much I love you. What is more wonderful in this life than love which has stood the test of time? Enjoy the simple things

of each day! We no longer need to revamp the church or change the world.

It is very helpful to be reminded to enjoy one day at a time.

A nurse at the Mayo Clinic assured Bob, "there will be more losses . . . but you will know—you will be able to pace yourself." She continues to affirm his judgment and values his input. Our local doctor does that, too. "You are an unusual Alzheimer's patient," he has told Bob, "knowing that you have the disease and being able to speak out. You are a help to us. Thank you!"

A well-meaning relative pummels us with questions we can't answer all at once: "Will you stay in your house? Will you have enough to live on? Have you been to a lawyer? Is there a support group in Grand Marais? Good nursing care? A hospice? Will the children help you? How long will this last?" Whoa! Don't raise too many questions all at once—especially if we haven't asked them ourselves. When we want your advice, we'll ask for it.

There are a few other things it is best not to say. Do not say that it is God's will. We believe in a God who wishes for all of creation health, wholeness, holiness (the same root word in Hebrew). Bob and I do not believe that we are being punished with his disease, or that people who live long lives are being rewarded by God for their good deeds.

Bob and I agree with the minister who preached, "Your fate has made you well." We worship a God who comforts us in times of suffering; we do not believe in a God who deals it out. We believe that God allows things to happen that God does not will. (We could not worship a God who intended the Holocaust or who wills the starvation of children throughout the world.)

Please do not imply that it is Bob's fault. He is not responsible for his disease because he did not run marathons or he used aluminum cookware for awhile or he did not take enough Vitamin E. No diet or exercise, no form of self-discipline can help anyone avoid Alzheimer's disease. The only thing that any of us might be able to do is choose our ancestors so that we do not inherit a very particular "bandit gene."

Do not pity us. "Pity is patronizing and debilitating," Bob says. We know that both patients and caregivers can become mired in self-pity and depression. According to the *World Book Dictionary*, pity means "a feeling of sorrow for someone who is suffering or in sorrow or distress, often felt to be weak or unfortunate." We are trying to be strong—not weak! Instead of pity, offer us compassion.

Do not say you know how we feel. No one can know for sure how someone else is feeling. Alzheimer's patients are not all the same.

Do not ask the question that wins our first prize for insensitive remarks: "Would Bob consider Dr. Kevorkian?"

Say almost anything to let us know you care. We will be grateful! Share your concerns with us that we may help you, too. All of us have pain to bear and it is because we recognize it that we can be "wounded healers," as Henri Nouwen says. Let's laugh and talk and cry together, acknowledging the wounds that bind us.

Our thirteen year-old granddaughter wrote:

> *I have some questions about alztimerzes disease but I just want you to know that I am not being mean or trying to hurt Bumpa's feelings. . . . But anyways, I was not sure if he still remembered me and I could not make up my mind if I should ask you. . . . Maybe you could send me some information on it—or not? Tell Bumpa I love him!*

I wrote back (enclosing some brochures from the Alzheimer's Association):

> *Dear Child,*
>
> *Of course he remembers! At some level, Bumpa will always remember. He loves you, too. Thank you for asking so we can tell you that.*

Robert Davis is a minister who was also afflicted with early-onset Alzheimer's disease. His experience is similar to Bob's. In his book, *My Journey into Alzheimer's Disease*, he writes about the early stage:

> I need more rest and recuperative time after social contacts. I may not remember your name, but if I have known you, I still know you. The disease interferes with access passageways especially to the names of things, but I still know the thing. It is the vocabulary, not the concept, that is gone at this early stage.
>
> As soon as my diagnosis was announced, some people became very uncomfortable around me. I realize that the shock and pain, especially to those who have a parent with the disease, are difficult to deal with at first. It was strange that in most cases I had to make the effort to seek out people who were avoiding me and look them in the eye and say, "I don't bite. I am still the same person. I just can't do my work anymore . . . I am still at home in here, and I need your friendship and acceptance."
>
> Usually the response was one of great relief. Over and over the answer came, "I'm so glad you said that. I just didn't know what to say. I didn't know how to treat you. I didn't know if you could still laugh."

C H A P T E R   S E V E N

Growing Down

JANUARY 20

Today Bob said, "I'm glad I went to Mayo. I'm glad I know. It helps me to understand. I used to have so much energy, so many dreams—too many to keep up with them all. I used to be so creative! Now . . . now, there is nothing."

He said it matter-of-factly. I argued with him, of course. Then I tried attentive listening.

"You feel discouraged."

"I'm not what I was," Bob replied.

"You miss those days."

"Oh, yes! I felt alive and useful then," he said, wistfully.

"You feel useless now?"

"Sometimes . . ."

I hugged him as long, as hard as I could. I reassured him how important he is to me, to his children and grandchildren. ("I hope they remember his birthday!" I thought.)

Bob turned 63 last week. We went to Duluth to celebrate his birthday by going to a touring production of *Cats*. When he was packing for the trip, he came upstairs.

"I'm not good at this . . . Come to think of it, I'm not good at anything. Can you help me?" Bob asked.

So I laid his clothes out on hangers—one set of clothes for each day. Three hangers to put in his garment bag: slacks, shirt, and sweater or sweatshirt on each one. "You could wear a turtleneck with this shirt," I suggested.

"What's a turtleneck?" he asked.

We put out belts and shoes. "Now all you need is your socks and underwear," I told him.

"Great! Thank you."

"And your toilet kit and pills," I added.

"Oh, yes . . . I have those all laid out."

But when we got to Duluth: no socks, no underwear or pajamas, no pills. He felt stupid, angry with himself, and worried that he would be cold in the night. I assured him that we could get some underwear in the morning, and I found an extra blanket. "You'll be fine," I told him. And he was fine, physically.

When we went to the play, Bob had to use the bathroom during intermission. The lobby was packed. "It's over there," I said and pointed.

"Come with me!" Bob urged, "wait here."

We got separated on the way back to our seats. I was leading. I turned around to talk to him, but he had drifted toward the back of the line. I stepped out of line to let him catch up. Then I saw the look of panic on his face.

"I couldn't find you! I don't know where our seats are."

"You have the ticket stub," I reminded him. "You could ask an usher to show you the seat." I said it as if I could teach him what to do in case he got lost some other time.

"Oh, yeah," Bob said, seeming to remember.

I almost wish he would get mad at me in times like this, even unreasonably mad as he might have done a year ago: "You didn't wait for me! I can't keep up with you! You got too far ahead. . . !" Anything. But instead, he meekly took my hand and followed me into the theater.

The next afternoon I went shopping. "I'll be back in an hour," I promised. "I'll look for you in the lobby. If you are not there, I'll come up to the room." I was fifteen minutes late. When I got to the room, Bob was pacing.

"How could you be gone so long? Almost three hours! I didn't know where you were. I waited and waited."

He had lost all sense of time and of place. He got lost on the way from the lobby to our room, and he had panicked.

He settled down after awhile, and we talked about precautions we can take when we travel: I will tell the clerks at the hotel desk if I go out alone, inform them where I will be, and when I expect to return. We will put the name and number of a local friend in Bob's wallet, and I will give that reference to the desk as well. We will be sure that Bob wears the necklace that identifies him as an Alzheimer's patient. We will also be sure he has his home address as well as the name and phone number of the hotel.

As we celebrated Bob's birthday, we had glimpses of what the year ahead may bring. I began to feel anxious every time we were separated. The kind of anxiety you feel when you leave a fourth- or fifth-grader home alone—first for an hour, then for two or three. Only it works backwards: Where once I felt free to leave home for a day or to leave the hotel for an afternoon, now I become uneasy within an hour. Is Bob comfortable? Will he be scared? If someone comes to the door, or calls on the phone, can he handle it? Will he get lost?

As we drove home from Duluth, Bob exclaimed, "Well! That was fun, wasn't it? At least most of it was fun."

JANUARY 26

An acquaintance of ours believes that her husband has Alzheimer's disease, but he won't admit it. She took him to the doctor, and she told me how pleased she was when the doctor told him that he was driving his wife "nuts!" What good did that do him, I wonder.

The wife exclaims, "How could he do this to me? We've always done everything together!" Then, immediately, she feels guilty, angry. "I know he can't really help it." I understand her conflicted feelings. She feels deprived. In *The Way of the Heart*, Henri Nouwen describes anger as a response to deprivation.

One day we met the couple in town for lunch. Bob was left concerned and frustrated by the meeting.

I thought I could help him, but his wife wouldn't let him talk to me. She talks all the time, doesn't listen, and is mad at him because he can't do what he did before. She's feeling sorry for herself, doesn't know where he's at, and he denies his illness. Well, of course he does. What else does he have left?

FEBRUARY 2

The sun is out! This is good news on the North Shore where we rejoice at "only six more weeks of winter" if the groundhog sees its shadow. Today is bone-chilling cold. By midday it hadn't warmed to minus 20 degrees Fahrenheit. The weatherman says warmth from the sun will "not be noticeable."

We have had three heavy storms in the last two weeks—snow piled on snow. The drifts are so high there seems no place to put any more of the white stuff. All over the county grown-ups are exclaiming, "This is like the winters I remember as a child . . . snow way over my head!"

We have been housebound, but there is enough food and firewood. We learned from blizzards on the farm to stockpile another staple—toilet paper. Our power has stayed on. We are warm and comfortable. We have gotten a lot of projects done. We sorted books, I organized my files, put photos in the albums, assembled tax records. We cleaned closets. I caught up on ironing. I have never finished my "winter list" before. The house is so neat and tidy it's almost frightening—like being ready to die.

I am ready for some disorder! I have been stricken with cabin fever. I want contact with people who lead messy, exciting lives. This morning, we talked about plans for the weekend. "I could make a big pot of soup," I proposed. "Why don't we invite someone for lunch Saturday or Sunday?"

"I don't understand it! You were gone all day Thursday!" Bob said, frustrated. "Isn't that enough? For you it's go-go-go! Everybody is more important to you than I am!"

I was home all day Monday and Tuesday. I was gone for about three hours on Wednesday to plan a workshop at the church, then for six hours on Thursday to lead it. I was home all day Friday with no plans for the weekend except church. How could I explain that for me the schedule was not "go-go-go"?

We were at an impasse. We couldn't work it out, fight it out, settle it. The irresistible need for social contact meets the immovable desire to stay at home alone. Again.

This afternoon I was on the phone. When I hung up and walked out of the kitchen, Bob called after me: "You don't want to talk to me, you just want to talk on the phone. The only people who are important to you are your women friends. You're always making plans—you can't bear to be cooped up with me!"

It's not true! I have enjoyed these amazing winter days. The sun dancing off bright snow cheers me when I do my household chores. The soft snowfalls and the long dark evenings comfort me while I read by the wood stove. Bob and I have listened to beautiful music, and we've had long, funny, sad conversations.

I feel blessed to share my life with this man. I wish he would believe that. I wish I could convince him I am not choosing between him and friends when I want to go out, talk on the phone, or invite people to come over. I do not seek to build a new and separate life for myself. My life is, and always will be, entwined with his. It grows on his support.

Love is not "either-or." It is "both-and." Bob knows this. He has preached the message for almost forty years. But he is lonely now and scared. His losses are profound. Patients in the early stages of Alzheimer's disease may become so disoriented to time and place that they focus on persons close to them and shadow their caregivers. I know that Bob's anger at me is mixed with envy because he can't go out much and because only a few people call him on the phone.

But I am lonely as well, and I'm scared of losing the friends on whom I shall most certainly depend. "It would be so good for Bob if you would get him out more," people urge me. Or even, "He brings the sickness on himself by staying home so much!" How can they understand?

In church recently, a member of the congregation asked Bob what he feels God is calling him to do. After a long pause he answered, "Endure."

Endurance. That's what this process is all about, isn't it? This aging thrown into fast forward by Alzheimer's disease. It is not a passive attitude, as once I thought, but rather a fierce, silent wrestling with change and compromise.

"Spring will come," I said to Bob late this afternoon. We looked outside. The sun that was "not noticeable" had cast some long shadows on the high white drifts. "Six weeks," I tried to reassure us both. "Just six more weeks?"

Gently, he took my hand. We stepped outside, breathed as deeply we could without freezing our lungs, then scurried back into the house to burrow in for the rest of winter.

FEBRUARY 7

Bob puts our personality differences into perspective:

Marriages work best when personalities are different, I think. Otherwise they can be boring. We need the stimulation that comes from contrast.

It isn't your contact with other people that bothers me. I want you to have that because you come home and share interesting things with me, and I get information about what is going on. I like that.

What I don't like is when you get real busy with other people and things to do outside the house, and so you get angry about all the things to do at home. Then you're not relaxed and loose, and we don't have as much fun.

Time after time, when you get harried it's because you're doing lots of running and not taking time to let your soul catch up so you can be at ease. It's a difficult balance. I need stimulation now—if I don't have enough I get depressed. On the other hand, I also can get depressed if there is more than I can handle.

FEBRUARY 12

Bob is feeling achy today—slow, tired, and sore for no obvious reason except, perhaps, it is February. The days are dark and cold, and angst is going around. But victims of chronic illness do not have the luxury of "feeling poorly." They dare not have an off day. They develop a hypersensitivity to their bodies. When Bob is tired, he wonders: "Is it getting worse?" If he has more than the usual trouble remembering, he asks, "Is my mind failing fast?"

I never before realized how lucky we are, we who can just take two aspirin and go to bed.

FEBRUARY 14

Today Bob and I met with Jan, our spiritual advisor.

There is a great tendency in me to focus on what I have lost, the things I can't do, the things I can't remember, etc. And this type of thought then leads me to become obsessed with losses and only be aware of what is dying—or disappearing or forgotten. Then I feel that everything good is dying— and I am dying.

One day as I was thinking of the losses, I could see myself becoming more childlike every day. When I am in an unfamiliar place and I can't find Anne, I panic just like I did when I was a small child in unfamiliar surroundings and couldn't find my mother.

As I was thinking of this apparent regression, and feeling sad about it, I thought about becoming a child. I recalled Jesus' words: "Unless you become as a little child, you will never enter the Kingdom of Heaven." I found this reassuring. Even if I am losing much of myself, I am not outside of God's love. I may be even closer than before.

I feel an urgency in each day to get projects finished, because I don't know how long I can do them. Anne and I have always exchanged valentines. This year I felt a real need to write something that would tell her how much I appreciate all of the extra work and responsibility she has assumed and how graciously she has done it. I wrote it out on paper. I checked and rechecked the spelling. I made some changes. It never said what I wanted it to say, so I would rewrite it and correct it. I wrote four or five lines— all told it took me about two and one-half hours to write a short note on the valentine. It came out pretty well, and I felt such an achievement!

When I can be grateful for what I can do, I feel good. When I concentrate on what I can't do—or do poorly—I feel bad.

CREATIVE INTERVENTIONS

Our local clinic sponsored a series of three videotaped lectures called "Creative Interventions for the Alzheimer's Patient." It was planned for caregivers, family members, professionals in various health-care fields, and interested members of the community.

Bob and I went to all three sessions. At the first meeting, when we went around the table and introduced ourselves, Bob said very quietly but firmly, "I was not invited as an Alzheimer's patient, so I am here as an interested member of the community."

"Oh!" several people exclaimed, clapping their hands to their mouths and shaking their heads. They apologized for not thinking to invite the patients. The thought had not occurred to them.

At the third meeting, Bob was asked by the professionals if he would be willing to stay on and talk about his personal experience of the disease. Many of them told him then, and have told us since, that his remarks taught them more than the series of lectures did.

The following is a compilation of Bob's responses to some of the questions from participants after viewing the video series:

At this point, I am anxious to share all I can about what it is like from the inside. I think of all the people who try to hide it and use all this energy . . . If we could just move to a place where having Alzheimer's is like having a stomach ache. Or if we could be like my three-year-old grandson who explains simply, "Bumpa? Oh, he's Alzie."

It's interesting . . . at first, people tried to keep me at arm's length—they didn't know what to say or do—but now I find more and more people say, "Well, that's just Bob, and he has Alzheimer's."

Otherwise it's like living with alcoholism—hiding things, denying, feeling shame. I see people having all sorts of difficulty remembering, but trying so hard to cover it up.

There is a lightness in knowing and sharing the truth. It helps others, and it also helps us to understand what is happening.

Bit by bit, there is a realization of the things I am losing. I can't get the word I want. I never used to have trouble talking, but now the words don't come up. I can't remember names. I have to work very hard to do something that I could do before without conscious effort. It's difficult to write—I can't remember how to spell words. I was good at math and I could work things out in my head. Now I find it hard—to work them out, to balance a checkbook, even to write checks.

I don't drive at night or in areas I don't know because in a situation where there are choices to be made, I tend to get panicked. I can't do two things at once. I can't recognize landmarks unless they are very familiar.

I carry a pad of paper with me with my name and address and telephone number. I spend quite a bit of energy trying to think ahead about what might happen—I can't rely on pulling things off at the last minute. And I have to try to get over the embarrassment when I don't know things or can't remember names.

I don't keep a calendar any more. Writing is hard and, if I did look at dates or appointments, I might not know what they meant. Reading is much slower. I read the newspaper every day, but I can't read handwriting at all. I still like having a wall calendar in my den to keep some sense of what time is, . . . and I like my watch. I want to keep wearing my watch, even if I have to ask someone to read it for me most of the time.

Often I feel like I am working backwards to earlier times. When I was little, I had to learn how to print letters. Then later I could do cursive writing. I learned how to add and subtract. I learned how to read signs, etc. . . . Now it works the other direction. Week by week I lose something I once learned at an earlier age. Things I could do almost by instinct now take a lot of effort. For instance, it's the hardest work to make a phone call. All those numbers . . . remembering who I am going to talk to . . . what to say . . . It didn't used to be so hard! But I want to keep doing it.

I get much more tired. Being with people wears me out, but I love it and need it, too. But if it goes on too long, I need to get away to a quiet place, put my head back, close my eyes.

After I do something that takes energy or after I eat, I often feel dizzy. So I go to my den and sit for awhile. It helps to listen to music—especially classical music. Then I get rid of that sort of pulling sensation in my head. I like to have my own room where I can go.

It works best if our routine is very simple. I like physical activity. I like doing work that is real: splitting wood, plowing snow. . . .

I have more difficulty dealing with anger in a constructive way than I once did. If somebody gets angry, or I feel they are angry, I feel it emotionally. Before, I could have worked it through my head and not taken it personally or reacted too much. I could have understood. Now, I have an emotional response that is less clear, and it takes me longer to set it in perspective. Meantime, I get more upset than I would have at one time.

The big obstacle to get over is that I am always aware of what I have lost. I feel different. I used to be defensive. Now I'm more able to think about what I still have. I'm feeling freer than I did, because I'm not trying to be the way I was before I had Alzheimer's. I can speak up. I can laugh, so it's easier for other people to put up with me.

If I can keep laughing, it's much more bearable. After all, life is terminal. I'm not so different from any one else, except that I probably know how I will die.

CHAPTER EIGHT

EARLY SPRING

APRIL 1

We had planned a vacation trip to Texas, but both of us were worried. Could I handle all of the details by myself? Would it be too confusing for Bob?

The most frightening thing about going away from home is that Bob and I both know that he is totally dependent on me. I, who am navigationally challenged, must do all the map reading and the driving, make all arrangements and try to do it without getting flustered or upset. But I can get lost so easily, feel stupid, get angry with myself. Then Bob reacts.

I can't help it. I pick up on your moods. When you get anxious, I get anxious!

Leaving the security of home and familiar surroundings, packing for summer weather when we were deep in winter, clearing the desk and arranging house care, planning our itinerary . . . it all seemed like too much trouble.

I'd rather stay home! I won't be able to do this again! It is so confusing. I just can't keep it all straight—it jumbles in my mind. I can't sort things out. I just can't.

We knew that when we got to Texas it would take Bob a few days to find his way around and get comfortable. A strange environment would frighten him.

I can't find my way around. I'm embarrassed to tell people what my problem is. I used to be able to laugh at myself when I got lost, but not any more . . . I worry about something happening to you. I don't want you to take risks. Don't go out by yourself—at least not too long . . .

I like being with take-charge kinds of people. They aren't scared of me. I can relax when others plan the outings as long as they aren't too long. People can't understand how I get so tired!

I don't know if we will have another vacation. I'll keep trying as hard as I can, but I notice changes . . . My balance isn't as good; I'm forgetting more . . . We used to make so many plans. Now I can't make plans. I can't even plan my own schedule.

We were nervous but excited as we took off for the month of March. The plane trip to Austin was my worst nightmare come true. We flew out of Duluth; because of an ice storm there, we missed our connections in Minneapolis-St. Paul. The next plane we could get on was delayed three hours for engine repair.

The Twin Cities' airport was crowded and noisy. We had to stay near our gate for updates on the plane's condition, but we had vouchers for snacks at the other end of the concourse. So we separated—one of us ate or went to the bathroom, the other waited by the gate. The milling crowds, constant muffled announcements from loudspeakers, the darkness . . . it was like something out of a Kafka story for me. Every time Bob was out of sight, I worried that we would not find each other. But he was fine. When we finally arrived at our hotel at 1:00 a.m., I asked him how he stayed so calm. "Easy!" he replied, "I don't have to worry. I'm not responsible here."

He is exhausted by crowds of people he knows—or should know—at church, concerts, or parties for instance. But an impersonal crowd does not bother him as long as he is with someone. If something should happen to his companion (a concern that is never far from my mind when we are away from home), he has cards in his billfold, and he wears a necklace identifying him as an Alzheimer's patient. I am scared of the responsibility sometimes, but I do not want either of us to be defined by our fears.

We learned a lot on this vacation. We learned that getting there was not half bad. We found out that Bob can thrive on a moderately active social schedule. We stayed in a resort community that was recommended by some friends from Grand Marais who just happened to be in the unit next door. They knew all the other "winter Texans" by the time we arrived, and they introduced us around. We were invited to join their "happy hours" if we wanted to; we were included in their golf foursomes and their potlucks, but we were never pressured to participate. Sometimes we joined them, most times not.

If the other guests knew about Bob's disease, we didn't know they knew. For the first time since the diagnosis, Bob was not "Bob with Alzheimer's," nor I "Anne the caregiver." Being honest about the disease, we realized that we have been both freed and imprisoned by it. People who know us observe carefully. What does Alzheimer's look like and act like? Whatever Bob does is attributed to or excused by his illness, and whatever I do, to the stress of being the caregiver. Bob wants to be just Bob . . . with foibles and talents, strengths and weakness.

In Texas, Bob thought that he was treated as he would have been anyway. It felt good. But people were especially kind to him, helping in unobtrusive ways: drawing maps of places to visit, including us in sightseeing trips and dinners out, answering Bob's questions matter-of-factly when he repeated himself.

There were strained times, of course (there always are on vacation), times when we felt displaced, lonely, even disloyal to our snowbound friends and family. "I don't feel useful here!" Bob exclaimed one day. But the lesson we learned, even from difficult days, is the therapy of laughter.

The resort complex was not well managed, and the guests took turns entertaining each other with stories about keys that didn't fit, phones that didn't work, the girl at the desk who couldn't make change from a dollar for a fifty-cent newspaper. When you are staying on someone else's property and the sewer backs up, it may be annoying and messy, but it is also funny. When the weather ruins your plans for the day and you have a whole month ahead of you, making an alternate plan is no problem.

The unfamiliar environment, the different foods, even the mannerisms of people in another part of the country are fascinating, provocative, and funny. Our experiences bonded us to the other visitors. We relaxed.

As we packed to leave, Bob looked around our small cluttered rental unit with its dirty dark blue carpet and unrelieved off-white walls.

"I will be sad to leave here. Do you think we will ever take another vacation? I've always wanted to go to Hawaii."

"You have? I didn't know that!" I exclaimed. I made a mental note to call our travel agent as soon as we got home.

On the plane back to the gray, frozen north, I began to think about gaudy crimson and yellow flowers, a clean apartment with a wide lanai, warm ocean breezes, new acquaintances . . . Could we afford it? Should we splurge now and invest in memories that will comfort us later, or should we be totally practical and save the money for future health care? A year from now would we even be able to travel?

"Let's go!" I said to Bob, as we unloaded suitcases and sorted the amazing accumulation of mail. He frowned. Hesitated. Then, pulling dirty laundry out of his duffel, he agreed, "Okay! Let's plan on it."

APRIL 3

You don't "get it" until you get it! You never realize until you see life through the eyes of an impaired person, howfast-peopletalktoeachother. Or how NOISY the world is, how stressful a walk around the block can be. The cacophony of voices, music, car horns . . . When you are s-l-o-w to distinguish words and sounds, when it takes a conscious effort to sort them out, a city environment can be toxic. I'm so glad to be back in Grand Marais!

APRIL 15

We drove to Wisconsin to spend Easter with Wayne's family. Then, one evening, we visited our old Koinonia study group in Amery—seven people from our church with whom we used to meet once a month. They are all good friends, but Bob was uncomfortable.

I feel that people are being nice to me because I have Alzheimer's. Part of it is, I don't really know what I am feeling—maybe it is all inside me. But before, when I was in a group, we had some pretty good evenings. Others not so good, but I was who I was; they were who they were.

But now, I worry that they seem shy around me. They are observing. Don't know what to say, I guess. I would like them to talk about it. I didn't know how to talk tonight. I feel badly because I didn't do my part, but I didn't know what my part was. I'm conflicted!

My biggest feeling is that I didn't do what would make me comfortable. I wish I had said: "We have known each other for a long time. I'm a little different, but not all that much. The difference is I'm diagnosed with Alzheimer's. I probably had it when you knew me before. Let me tell you what is happening to me and clear the air . . ." I feel best when I feel loose.

APRIL 23

Bob's childhood friend came from Seattle to visit. She and her siblings participated in an Elderhostel at Lutsen Resort, and we spent two delightful evenings together.

"I'm so relieved!" she exclaimed to me. "He seems just the same." People who see Bob after a long time always remark on how well he looks. "I was nervous about it," they say. What they can't realize is how hard Bob tries, how much effort it takes for him to seem "just the same," how tired and confused he gets after a period of trying to keep up with conversations and reminiscing.

The effort is good for him. He basks in the feelings of care and concern, in the laughter and the memories, reinterpreted, pieced together, and handed back to him.

There was a dance on the last evening of the Elderhostel. "I'm too stiff," Bob said as we drove to Lutsen. "I can't dance . . . could never follow the instructions." But when the lively music started it was easy to pull him out on the floor.

Bob surprised me, Lila, her sisters, and members of the band by dancing every number! "Twinkletoes," we teased him. And if he "do-si-do-ed" when he was supposed to "see-saw," or he balanced right when it should have been left, what did it matter—except that he got a kick in the shin. "Let's face it, Bobby," Lila laughed with him. "You weren't the best dancer in high school either."

APRIL 27

Finally, we started sorting the barn! It was a beautiful spring day. Streams were tumbling down hill into the pond, and snowdrifts were melting into puddles on the driveway. There was not much open ground after our record-setting winter, but the sun was warm, and the barn felt comfortable to work in when we opened the big doors on the south side.

We walked down there together. Bob was overwhelmed at the sight of all the boxes to be opened, at all the piles of stuff covering the workbench, at the tools strewn around the floor.

"I don't know where to start. Do you have any ideas?"

I gasped. I don't know a washer from a nut. I can barely distinguish a nail from a screw. I didn't have any ideas at all about what most of these things were or how to organize them. Bob wanted his workshop in order. I had come to help him, both for moral support and with the hope that I would gain space in the barn for gardening supplies.

"Honey, I can help you with your closet, and I can sort your books, but I can't make decisions here. You tell me where you want things, and I'll put them there."

"This is too much! I can't do it. I'll never be able to use this stuff anyway. I'm ended," Bob said in frustration.

"Well, you don't need all of it . . . let's just save out what you want."

"I can't! I don't even know what it is anymore."

Bob was dizzy. He put his hand on the right side of his forehead where it always seems to hurt when he gets anxious. He sat down on the stairs. Then he stood up and walked back to the house.

I had no choice. I started opening little brown paper bags, dozens and dozens of little brown bags: nails—long nails, short nails, galvanized nails, headless nails, regular nails; gizmos in heavy wire that looked like giant hairpins; brads— 1/2", 3/4", 7/8" brads in tiny plastic tubes; blue "whatchamacallits" that seemed to go with screws; "thingamajigs" for changing motor oil or patching tires.

I sorted together things that seemed to look alike and put them in the storage boxes Bob had mounted on the wall. Four hours I stood on the spring-cold concrete floor. But by the end of the afternoon, all the little paper bags were ready for recycling, and four or five cardboard cartons had been emptied as well.

Bob is very quiet tonight. Sullen. He doesn't want to talk. He doesn't feel well physically or emotionally. He is grieving for his workshop, for the dreams he had of building there. The barn was "his" space.

"This is a terrible day. I wish I could just shovel it all out for you. I don't know what to do when I've got it, and I don't know how to get rid of it!"

"Keep it for now. The boys may want it some day . . . or we can have a yard sale," I offered.

He doesn't need the advice I give him. I know that. He just wants me to listen, but I'm afraid I'll cry.

We both know that all this work may be wasted. Bob will do household repairs and little projects for as long as he is able, but he will never assemble his table saw. All the nails and the screws, the nuts and bolts, neatly arranged in their little storage boxes, will probably just gather dust. The tools, hung on the wall, laid on shelves Bob built, or put away in his tool chest, will be loaned, given away, or sold. But we will sort them out anyway.

MAY 19

"Depression is sometimes a symptom of Alzheimer's disease," the erudite young research doctor told us the other day at a workshop for caregivers. Why in the world wouldn't it be? A man has been told that he has a disease for which there is no cure. He will lose his mental capacity and his physical coordination. He will forget his past. He will not comprehend present reality, and for him there will be no future, no dreams. He will become a burden to himself, his family, and his community.

He could live this way for twenty years. Of course he will be depressed. Maybe he has had periods of depression for several years, has been suspicious of the symptoms that led him to the doctor's office. Does this sound abnormal? Psychotic? "We need to intervene," says the doctor, "and treat depression aggressively." NO! Not unless this man is a danger to himself or others.

The patient must enter into this dark night if he is ever to emerge into a light of new hope, new being. Let him go. Say a prayer for him. His family and friends will walk with him as far as they are able, but they, too, may become depressed. They are not ill though, indeed, they are diseased. Respect their feelings! Don't even imply that they are weak or sick because they feel shock, grief, and terrible black sadness. Don't try to take their feelings away by distraction or medication.

When we came home from Rochester I had great, heavy bouts of depression. I lost ten pounds because I wasn't hungry and couldn't sleep. I felt dull. Life seemed flat. Everything, everyone was too much work. I forgot to do things: return phone calls, attend meetings, even pay bills. I could not pray. Eventually, the black mood lifted, but the depression did not go away until it had come full circle. Depression is a cocoon, wrapping new life in layers and layers of lost dreams.

The doctors who want to cure everything, but cannot cure Alzheimer's disease, try to fix the depression that comes with it.

I want to fix it, too! I want to hold Bob and kiss the hurt and make it go away. But, sometimes, all I can do is detach. I can sit with him, if he wants me to, and let him cry. Let the black mood come. I can try to remove myself emotionally—after all, it is his pain and he is entitled to it. But I must not go too far away physically. I have learned in the past year just how easily Bob can feel abandoned.

Today I was helping him assemble a firewood holder: two-by-fours screwed into four metal brackets, one for each corner. It took us all afternoon. In frustration, Bob began to sob. He put his hand on the right side of his forehead.

Right here. It hurts—it clouds up—right here. I can see it . . . then I can't. Can't remember why . . . what I'm doing. What's wrong with me? Sometimes I think I could just go to bed and wake up in the morning and be all normal again. I think people with Alzheimer's just give up because everything is so much work!

CHAPTER NINE

Speaking Up

Since Bob was diagnosed with Alzheimer's a year ago, he and I have experienced all the emotions that surround any kind of death: first denial, then bargaining, anger, and depression, then a grudging acceptance. Unfortunately, they are not experienced in a tidy order, and with each loss the cycle begins again. Sometimes we go round in circles and make no progress at all. Other times we are simply inundated by feelings we cannot sort out or even name. We have wrestled with them this last year. Like Jacob of the Old Testament, we are limping; like him, we have been blessed.

We are blessed, first of all, by knowing the name of the angel-demon with whom Bob is struggling: Alzheimer's disease. Walter Wangerin, Jr., writes about the importance of knowledge in *Mourning into Dancing*:

> Knowledge, even the difficult knowledge of the sources of sorrow, is always an advantage. Always. Knowledge itself may not change things. To know what truly has caused your sadness may not abolish the sadness. But it is the beginning of comfort: you have named the thing. You have sought the cause and found it; it is no longer hidden. The real thing is before you. Now, knowing its name and its character . . . you may yourself begin to participate in its healing. (82)

Bob says, in different ways, that it has been healing to know. How much easier it is to be honest with yourself and others! We can take an active stance with grief, share what we learn and what our experience has been. To be passive is, as one grief counselor says, to "get beaten up by it."

Another way that we are blessed is in our relationship. Closer than ever after 25 years of marriage, we feel we have been strengthened by each test along the way. Not that we would choose the testing! Far from it. I was brought up on sentiments of "happily ever after." But life is far harder, far more complicated, and much more beautiful than we understood when we were young.

We have been blessed by our family. Bob's sons, struggling with their own grief and anger, have grown in their ability to nurture him and to help each other; they are absorbing now many lessons that they were taught from childhood: no, life is not fair; yes, God is good. Nice young men are maturing into responsible adults by experiencing the very kind of pain all of us would like to spare our children. Bob's extended family is unfailing in its love and support for us both.

We have been blessed by friends here in our new community of Grand Marais and those scattered around the country as well: friends from school days, from other places we have lived and churches we have served.

We have been blessed with spiritual guidance from clergy who are friends and from friends who are ministers. We need to be constantly challenged to keep this journey in a spiritual perspective!

We have been blessed by excellent medical care both here and at the Mayo Clinic and by support services in a small community that cares and listens and tries to work together to serve its citizens.

We have been blessed by the beautiful environment in which we live—by the salving, inescapable presence of Lake Superior, the beauty of the rocks and trees, the teeming life of our north woods. Recently, a moose and two calves spent the morning in our driveway, then bedded down for an afternoon nap in our dogwood bushes. They watched us through the window. We feel very connected to the natural world.

We have had bad days. No doubt we will have more. They are part of the process of living with this disease. But only part. It would not be truthful to skip over the dark times, but it is not right, either, to weight them too heavily. It is important to know that between these entries, between the lines of every day are sandwiched light and happy hours:

> Gracious God, we pray that, living with disease, we may celebrate wellness. That in times of despair, we may find hope. That in fear, we may find faith. As we sing Bob's song, may it be in tune with all that is good and healthy and generative in your creation. May it be music for others to follow if they journey into the wilderness of Alzheimer's' disease, whistling to keep away the spirits of darkness.

MAY 25

Last week we went back to the Mayo Clinic for Bob's yearly evaluation in their research program. The prognosis was good. So far the disease is progressing slowly. So slowly, in fact, that the doctor spent more time talking to us about Bob's autopsy than about the results of the tests! In effect, what he said was that they had not learned enough from him, so far, to justify their expenses; he wanted to be sure that their research would benefit from Bob's death.

We understand by now that the focus of research programs must be statistics, data; they are seeking treatments or cures. Bob wants to help them. So do I. But all in due time.

"Join an Alzheimer's support group," the nurse urges Bob, forgetting again that the nearest one is 106 miles away. "Give the patient power over his own life," she tells me. It's an oxymoron. I am not God. I can't *give* Bob something he already has! But what I could do—what I must be ever diligent *not* to do—is to take power away.

The tests show that physical and spatial concepts are more difficult for him now. The short test for mental status was 31 out of 38 last year. Now it is 28 out of 38.

I understand what they tell me. I know the losses. These are hard . . . I guess they will all be hard.

Losses *are* hard. But I think we are more accepting now than we were on our last trip to Rochester. We have become accustomed to labels: "patient" and "caregiver." We understand our role as mentors to others who may be afflicted. We speak up for the rights of Alzheimer's patients. Living as gracefully as we can with the disease has become our cause. It will not get better. Alzheimer's does not go away; it is our constant companion. We have to learn to get along together.

JUNE 14

When Alzheimer's disease first came to our house, I treated him as an intruder. I say "him" because the disease is too personal to be an "it" and because he has visited the man in our household. This stranger had entered our private space against our will. He knocked down all the pretenses we erected against him, kicked in the doors, broke the locks. There was no one we could call to remove him. He was rude and too demanding to be ignored. I fumed against him. I resented his presence. I refused to give him space. But gradually, over the first year, I began to see him as a guest—uninvited, to be sure, and unwelcome. But he was here, and I had no choice but to give him room.

At first, it was just a little corner of the house. Soon it was a whole floor. Maybe if I am nice to him, I told myself, he will get tired and go away. He didn't, of course. The disease is more than a guest now; he is a resident. He eats at our table; he haunts our dreams; he is there every morning when we wake. I am finally realizing that the only choice left to me is to befriend him. Henri Nouwen writes about creating space for strangers in his book *Reaching Out*:

> If there is any concept worth restoring to its original depth and evocative potential, it is the concept of hospitality. It is one of the richest biblical terms that can

deepen and broaden our insight in our relationships to our fellow human beings. Old and New Testament stories not only show how serious our obligation is to welcome the stranger in our home, but they also tell us that guests are carrying precious gifts with them, which they are eager to reveal to a receptive host. (66)

The challenge to the host, to all of us who live perforce with illness and disease, is to learn to be receptive. To see what gifts the guest is bringing. Bob understood this months ago when he began talking about the "blessings" of Alzheimer's.

JUNE 30

Bob and I were in Duluth a few weeks ago to do some errands and get our big city "fix." We left early in the morning, drove for two hours, spent the day shopping and going to the dentist. We had a late supper at our favorite restaurant and walked back to our hotel on the beautiful boardwalk by Lake Superior. We were tired! I flipped on the television as I got into my nightgown. Quite by accident, we encountered a panel discussion of Alzheimer's disease on the Larry King show.

Between commercial breaks—ironically for products designed to keep us immortal, forever young, and healthy—the panel elaborated on the devastation of Alzheimer's: "It's a tragic way to go." "Could there be anything worse?" "There is tremendous pain." "Families are torn apart!"

Dr. Zaven Khachaturian, director of the Ronald and Nancy Reagan Research Institute in Chicago, was on the show. "The baby boomers are in good health, and Alzheimer's is the one disease they can't prevent," he warned. "If we don't find a cure, the whole country—not just families—could be broke." There are four million people in this country who have been diagnosed with clinically probable Alzheimer's disease. "The tip of the iceberg," Dr. Khachaturian said.

It is the nature of talk shows, of course, to dwell on the dramatic. But shining such a bright light on all the suffering of Alzheimer's will drive even further into the shadows of medical and social isolation the very people who would be most able to help with research! Patients in the early stages are articulate and responsive. But why should they come forward after seeing a program like that?

As the panelists acknowledged, Alzheimer's is, indeed, a tragic way to go. But many of the early years can be productive. People may live with the disease for twenty years or more. They do not deserve to be isolated all that time.

A responsive and compassionate society would include these victims, listen to them, respect and challenge and learn from them. Responsible journalism would focus on their courage, their achievements, as well on their struggles. A responsible government would seek to lift the staggering burden of health care costs, encouraging communities to develop creative and less expensive models of housing and care.

It is not right that someone like Bob can pay for health insurance for himself and his family for more than forty years, and then have no assistance when he needs it. Nursing care for Alzheimer's patients, at home or institutionalized, costs $30,000 to $50,000 a year! It is not covered by Medicare or by private insurance policies.

One of Bob's colleagues has Alzheimer's. After paying for her husband's nursing care, his wife has $19.99 a month left over from their pensions and Social Security. She moved in with her daughter so she could sell her house and pay living expenses from the proceeds. She worries that she will live too long and have to go on federal assistance.

It is not right to expect people to be productive members of society while they are healthy, and then to isolate them physically, emotionally, and socially when they are diseased. The other day we met a teenager wearing a black T-shirt that announced in neon colors: "If you don't live on the edge, you take up too much room!"

Both of us were deeply distressed when our national church reported on a couple who willed the denomination $1 million and then committed suicide rather than "waste" their money on health care for her Alzheimer's. They were called brave, valiant, self-sacrificing.

There are serious issues—financial, social, ethical issues—that we need to wrestle with individually and in our communities. There is bad news about Alzheimer's that is easy to find. Someday there will be a cure for this devastating disease. But we need to hear and tell and search out stories of hope in the meantime.

And we need patients like Bob who are willing to come forward, model coping skills, and speak about their experiences with Alzheimer's disease. A woman I met in town recently asked, "Does Bob know how many people are watching him to see how he handles this?" People *are* watching. Many want to see and hear about Alzheimer's patients who live gracefully with this dread disease.

In Duluth today, we saw some paper napkins in a store window. The napkins had "Forgetfulness is next to Godliness" printed on them. Bob went in and bought the whole stack. "You never know where I might use these!" he said, chuckling.

One of the terrible things about this disease is the way it is often hidden. When people begin to believe they have the disease, they hide it and refuse to have it diagnosed. This is destructive to the person. It creates a terrible feeling of wondering, "What is wrong with me?"

I have found that most people have been extremely helpful when they know what the situation is. My criticism of the TV show is that all the people on the show were friends or relatives of people with Alzheimer's, but there were no people who have the disease.

We need someone with the courage to invite Alzheimer's patients who are able to speak for themselves onto programs. I know there are people with Alzheimer's who could articulate their concerns and tell others what it is like and how they would like to be treated. I believe that this could make for an exciting program and do a lot to help others understand the disease in the person, and even more, to know the person in the disease.

CHAPTER TEN

THE GIFT OF PRESENCE

When Bob told his sister that he had been diagnosed with Alzheimer's, he reassured her "something good will come out of this." He has always believed that there must be a purpose to his illness. Not that God visited it on him for any reason, but that God is the *ease* in his dis-ease, the Balm in Gilead.

In *Turn over Any Stone*, Edna Hong writes about living with pain and suffering and about confronting it:

> The mystery of pain and suffering can only be answered with a life that refuses to despair, refuses to hand one more victory to the forces of No, but instead makes itself an instrument of Yes, gives itself in love and compassion to alleviate pain and suffering.

JULY 2

Jan, our friend and spiritual advisor, said to him today, "Bob, even though you are an expert in the use of words and have depended on your skill at using them in your vocation, I experience you primarily as a presence. You are not a human doing or saying; you are a human being . . ."

It's true. Bob's presence is comforting, and lighthearted. You can feel his spirit, now as before. A man in the Bible study group that Bob attends occasionally urges Bob to come more often. "Your attitude is an inspiration to the rest of us!" he has said to Bob.

I told Jan that I, in contrast to Bob, have always had a tendency to do more than to be. I was the kind of mother who would do laundry before playing with the baby and correct grammar when children were telling me stories. (I'm better as a grandmother. Last week I sat through a tale told by our 12-year-old grandson and barely twitched to "me and him don't gots none"!)

I explained to Jan that I set the table for company the night before; I wash windows when the first maple leaf turns red. I service cars on schedule, pay bills promptly, make lists . . . and I irritate the rest of my family by assuming the role of "designated worrier."

"What does that give you?" she asked gently.

"Hmmmm . . . I can be busy, self-absorbed, even heroic," I responded.

"Avoid contemplation?" Jan prodded me.

"Hmmmm. . . ."

Perhaps I do run around the edges of my pain to avoid the center of it. Maybe I do pull away from Bob. I take over his tasks, projecting ahead—always ahead—to the time when Bob will not be here and, in the process, I shut him out.

I know you're busy now. You have so much to do. And I can't even help you! Do you remember when we first met— how we would just *be* together? We'd talk and laugh and not really do anything.

JULY 5

The Hebrew people in the wilderness were fed by manna, a miraculous substance that appeared with the morning dew and distilled by noon. Bob says Alzheimer's patients must live like those pilgrims.

I have to live in the here and now. I can't remember the past, and if I do, it makes me sad. I don't know the future, and I can't hoard present experience to use later. Today is a good day. I will celebrate that.

HERE AND NOW
We have this day—
this afternoon—
to sit on black ledgerock
splintered from mountains,
smoothed and polished by centuries
of wind and rain and ice.

We have this hour
to look at the lake
where blue-dappled waves
break the sun
into tiny stars
and sprinkle them
at our feet.

All we can know of mountains
is this warm, wet rock.
All I can see of sun
is in this star-drenched time,
here with you.

—Anne Simpson

JULY 8

Sometimes I get scared—when I can't do things. I look around and see all the things I used to do . . . it seems not long ago. It goes so fast. I look in the mirror. I seem just the same. How can I be different?

JULY 12

I suppose there is no woman who is satisfied with the way she looks—until she doesn't look that way any more: legs too short, waist too thick, hair too straight, too curly, wrong color. We discount our bodies, or we take them for granted.

If we are healthy, we trust them to take us where we want to go, to put up with our neglect or abuse and to function smoothly. Like a new car under lifetime warranty. And so we are surprised when the first symptoms occur—those funny little noises that signal arthritis, the extra thump in the engine that indicates heart disease . . .

Over time, the body that kept us light and mobile becomes heavy, a burden—something our spirit, now grown strong and independent, must lug around. Our physical being is something to cover, not to dress—something to put up with, be put off by, soon to be put away. The body may seem like a wrinkled barrier to others.

If we see this deterioration of the body and feel regret for it, how would the mind be any different? For over sixty years Bob's brilliant mind has served him. He took it for granted that he would be able to understand concepts and explain them, figure out solutions to almost any problem.

When I look at my own aging, when I see and feel weaknesses in my body, it makes me sad . . . and then ashamed. After all, what am I losing, compared to what Bob will lose? Like all other women my age, I am losing looks and strength. I am also losing dreams. But Bob, unlike most of his contemporaries, must let go of self. Yet he asks so little of me, his short legged, straight-haired wife—only that I love him and show that I do, even as he slips from me to become Bob no longer.

JULY 13

I have read that caregivers talk to others about their situations when they want either pity or praise. Over and over again I ask myself, "Is that true?" (Is that why I write?)

I was invited to a special meeting of the Caregivers' Group in Grand Marais. The pastor at the Lutheran church did a presentation on loss and grief. The group was small—six or seven. Most of the participants cared for spouses who were victims of strokes or of cancer. The facilitator, Julie, is a woman in her early forties, who has a son disabled by a rare muscular disease.

There were very sad stories embodied in that room at the Social Services Building. Pastor John often deferred to the caregivers as experts on the subject of grief. And yet there was laughter. There was hope, as people shared their stories, as they asked for and received advice and support. Sometimes the help was practical, sometimes emotional, often spiritual.

This was not what I expected in a support group! I had expected that we would take turns "dumping" all our problems on the group. Or that we would have a pity party, taking turns criticizing and complaining about the patients in our care. What I found instead was a group of very nice people who faced their problems realistically and tried to help each other make the best of them.

Julie, caring and friendly, keeps in touch with each group member, and she has kept them connected to one another. She plans social outings, sometimes with patients as well. She was as concerned for Bob as she was for me.

I need not feel guilty for going to a Caregiver's meeting. The group asked me to please come again. Much to my surprise, I think I will.

JULY 17

You didn't take me seriously. I told you that I felt awful.

For three days Bob had been exceptionally tired, felt weak and light-headed. I assumed it was Alzheimer's and he, too, worried that he was rapidly getting worse. Then he discovered blood in his stool. Aspirin, we decided. He had been taking it for arthritis. He had taken about ten coated tablets in the last week.

It was Saturday morning—of course. The clinic was closed. We decided to stop the medication, wait and call on Monday if he did not feel better. "Come in tomorrow," the nurse said. So Tuesday afternoon Bob saw the doctor. After his hemoglobin was tested, he was immediately hospitalized!

After two blood transfusions and an overnight stay, he was released, only to be sent to Duluth on Thursday. His blood count was still too low. The doctors knew it was internal bleeding. But where? Had it stopped? He was given another transfusion, pumped full of barium from top and bottom, x-rayed, and finally dismissed. He was limp, sore, and discouraged as we packed him to go home.

What did I do wrong?

Bob is so apt to blame himself. The doctor, the nurses, and I reassured him again and again that the bleeding was not his fault. He had an extreme reaction to aspirin that could never have been predicted. It had no connection to the Alzheimer's disease.

There is a lesson here that we have learned the hard way. One cannot assume that all symptoms of distress can be traced to Alzheimer's. Bob will have other health problems, just like anyone else his age. He is just as susceptible as the rest of us are to colds and flu, cancer and heart disease, bug bites, cataracts, and tooth decay. He deserves to have his symptoms studied objectively and to have his feelings respected, even if a time comes when he cannot express them clearly.

AUGUST 10

Bob sat at the dining room table this morning with a large notepad in front of him, pencil in hand.

"Can you help me?" he asked. "I get so confused! I want to write down all the chores I have to do this fall. I need to put them in order. Otherwise, I get so indecisive that I don't start anything."

I told him that his list looked pretty complete. He seemed relieved.

You tell me what to do! You plan the days for me so I can have a job and do it and feel good afterwards. There is something freeing about saying "I need help"—sometimes it seems ridiculous to a normal person, it's such a simple thing. But it's like seeing things—I can look right at them and not see them.

It is easier now that I know. The bad times were when I knew something was wrong but wouldn't admit it. I certainly wasn't thinking of Alzheimer's. You'd ask me to do something . . . I wasn't trying to be difficult, but I couldn't do it and wouldn't tell you, and we'd argue. Now you help me.

AUGUST 24

Yesterday Bob wanted to mow the hill behind our house, and he needed me to be with him when he used the big tractor—to watch for rocks and holes where he could drop a wheel, to give advice on where to cut. So I stayed home. There were a few twinges of self-pity, I'll admit. I had been invited to join a group of women for blueberry picking, and I had looked forward to the excursion.

But it was a golden day for Bob and, in the end, I was glad I could share it with him. It was the perfect weather of late summer. He had a task to accomplish before the days turned dark and cold. He did it well.

"Look at that hill!" he said and smiled proudly, wiping his forehead and pointing his grass-streaked seed cap in the direction of his mowing. Included in his wave were the brilliant blue sky, the gentle breeze, and the trees just turning.

"We won't have many days like this!" he beamed.

AUGUST 26

I like your enthusiasm. It's so nice that you'll say, "Let's go mow the grass!" You make it sound both interesting and exciting, so it makes me want to do it and think I can.

Before I had Alzheimer's, I could see things for myself and go do them. Now you have to see them. I can do them, if you tell me exactly what to do. That's a real gift you give me—tell me one thing, and I'll do it. Then you have to tell me something else.

I was having a terrible time with the mowers. You suggested that Dan come and you wrote down his instructions. By the middle of the summer, we were really doing well.

There are even times when I can get the mower going by myself! You do that often. Maybe you can't do something, but you think of someone who can. I can still drive the tractor because Mitch comes and helps me. I run all the lawn machines because Dan services them. When I'm not able to handle machines any more, I know I can count on Leonard. He's always so willing to help! I'm cautious, that's probably a plus. I'll know when I can't handle it any more.

People are good here about helping me, and they still treat me like I'm the same person. I'm dependent on Mitch and Dan and Leonard, but they still respect me. They charge a fair price for their help—if they didn't, I'd tell them.

AUGUST 28

We played golf at Silver Bay, an unfamiliar course about an hour away. Bob did not do well. It was hot, very humid, and he had only a few good shots.

"Golf is how I measure my deteriorating," he said, feeling discouraged. "I have more trouble now finding clubs, finding my ball. I feel weak."

I urged him not to jump to conclusions. It could be the weather, maybe he was just tired . . . everybody has bad days on the golf course. That's what keeps us coming back—maybe next time will be better.

So on he trudged. He tries so hard it almost makes me cry! He reads golf magazines, watches matches on TV, spends hours at the driving range—I could never have his patience or persistence!

"I'll never get any better," he admits. "No matter what I learn, I'll just forget again."

He will forget. And yet he goes back out, asking me to teach him if I can, to play more than I really want to play.

Our friends in the Couples' League are very patient and understanding. They help me keep his score. They laugh with him if he duffs a shot, and they celebrate when he hits a good one. Mostly retired people, they can afford to spend time on the course, and they have learned not to take the game too seriously.

There is Russell who plays four to five times a week, despite two heart attacks and back surgery; Gene, who gulps Tylenol to control the pain in his legs; Thelma, who gets out of breath walking up to the greens because of emphysema; and Roy, who had a foot amputated. "I expect I've earned a higher handicap," Roy once told his partners. "Not on your life," Russell responded. "With your new foot you can kick a ball anywhere, and it will really fly!"

I admire their perspective. I have always had a love-hate relationship with the game of golf. It is frustrating, expensive, and time-consuming. But I want to laugh with these friends, to treasure these days—lost balls, high scores, bugs, and all. I treasure them for the freedom we have, for the chance to exercise and to be outside, for the games we play (no matter how slow and awkward), and for the kind, good-humored people we meet. Who knows how much longer Bob and I will be able to walk together through thick green grass (and brambly woods), chasing a little white ball into a hole in the ground?

"You'll remember that it was fun, won't you? Remember that playing golf with me was fun?" Bob asked me.

LABOR DAY

Today we went to a picnic. I heard Bob talking to Zeke, expounding his newly-developed "theology" of golf to this non-believer.

To be human we keep creating meaning-givers. Theologically we know that they are empty, but most of them are less obvious than this game. They give a temporary kind of meaning—the danger is when we make them into reality. When we have faith in our own creations and not in God.

The nice thing about golf is that it can be a meaning-giver, but we can still see the silliness of walking around and hitting a little white ball. A sense of humor helps in our perspective. We all need to do things we think are important. I know golf is not that important, but it entertains us, gives us company and exercise, makes us feel good (at least sometimes), and it provides challenge. But when taken too seriously, it is a great disappointment.

SEPTEMBER 6

Most mornings Bob pads around in his robe and slippers until after breakfast, which he likes to eat in two installments: tea and toast when he first gets up, then oatmeal (with raisins and brown sugar) about an hour later.

This morning he was dressed early. Showered and shaved before the oatmeal course, he was grinning. "They asked me to help!" Bob said. Pete had called last night. He told us that they were laying new carpet at the church. Pete wondered if Bob could help them move some pews.

After breakfast I drove Bob into town, did a few errands, then came home. About an hour later the phone rang. "Come and get your hubby." He was waiting by the front door. He was very tired. But Bob smiled broadly when Pete said to me, "We gave him a workout. He carried a lot of heavy furniture. He's really strong!"

Sometimes people are hesitant to ask Bob for help. They don't want to bother him or to impose. They think he has enough problems already. But helping others is not a problem—it is a privilege. When Bob is asked to contribute his time and energy, he feels valued. Next week he will help Jack stack wood. He is already looking forward to their day together. I bet he'll get dressed as soon as he's had his tea!

CHAPTER ELEVEN
"What Do You Do All Day?"

It seems inevitable that when people meet for the first time, after they have been apart for awhile, they ask each other, "So, what have you been doing?" I have always hated that question! My mind goes blank. I don't know. "Nothing," I think, "nothing spectacular." So when I am asked that hated question now, I turn the conversation to our family or community news or the weather. On the North Shore, we can always talk about the weather.

I ran into a friend in town the other day. "Hi, stranger!" she greeted me. "I haven't seen you in ages. What have you been doing—gadding about?" A thoughtless comment, nothing more. But I was tempted to say, "Caregiving—that's what I do. It's a full-time job!" She doesn't want to know the details, and I don't want to bore or burden her. When Bob is asked what he has been doing, he would like to answer, "I have Alzheimer's. That's enough." It defines his days. But how can he explain?

Pat and Tom are a well-known couple in our community. Tom was recently diagnosed with Alzheimer's. Pat was immediately identified "caregiver" by their doctors. "It was as if I went out the window. Suddenly I wasn't me anymore!" Pat has said. She was just a person with a function: get affairs in order, seek legal advice, find services, plan to move and, in the process, maintain a normal life for herself and her family.

Bob says that Alzheimer's patients also feel invisible. Maybe Tom felt that he, too, was disappearing under a pile of things to do.

Pat and Tom sent a letter to their employees, alerting them to the diagnosis. It was a very moving letter, their openness and honesty was respected. People in town talked to each other about the situation, of course, but not many of them talked to the patient or the caregiver. "That's okay," says Pat, "though it would be nice if people talked more openly about Alzheimer's."

Pat, like me, was a stay-at-home mom. We didn't "work." So we dreaded the question, "What did you do all day?" I wanted to justify myself. Sometimes I still do. But Pat is wiser. She says, "My days were too important to explain. They still are. If you don't understand parenting you will never understand caregiving. We are put to work by God."

The other day I was filling out a form that asked my occupation. For the first time I wrote "caregiver" instead of "homemaker" or "retired," and I felt satisfied with the answer. That same night a full moon rose above Lake Superior. It was so bright and garish that I called Bob to come outside. We stood together silently for a long, long time. Caregiver. Patient. That's what we do. That's who we are. It is enough.

SEPTEMBER 8

A call from an old friend:

"Hello . . . How are you, Bob? Sorry I haven't called sooner, but you know our family. We're all workaholics.

"I made jelly this week, went to my daughter's and put up quarts of dill pickles (the family loves my pickles, you know), went to the Senior Center and played the piano for an hour and a half (they clapped after every piece). I taped the service at church, took it to my neighbor's, then I baby-sat my granddaughter . . . So you can see, I'm busy. See how busy I am? Even in my seventies, I guess I can still be useful! So, Bob, what have you been doing? Hello? Bob?"

I'm still here.

SEPTEMBER 10

Bob and I were talking about the church this morning, about how we could contribute to the Christian education program, how we could work with the minister and committees. I told him how much he helps me. In this case, how he clarified my thinking about the Christian education program and helped me outline a plan of action. He was pleased.

"Call the council president," Bob said. "I want to explain how I think it could work."

I called and left a message; tonight she called back. We were watching TV when the phone rang. I answered. "It's for you . . . Cathy. She's returning your call." Bob looked blank. I told her he might call her back. After doing the dishes, I went downstairs. Bob was sitting quietly in the dark.

I live in two worlds. Sometimes I can function. Sometimes I just can't. I know I have something to offer and I want to share it, but I'm afraid I'll get stuck . . . I want to be able to help! Do I help you?

What will happen if I don't have something I can do? I don't want you to remember me as a burden. I'm so afraid you'll get disgusted or worn out . . . I feel badly that I can't be strong for you.

SEPTEMBER 12

The clergy of our Association met today in Grand Marais. Bob got up early to shower and dress for his meeting with the other ministers in our area. I packed his lunch, called him when it was time to go. He walked upstairs from his den. I turned to smile at him. My face fell, I know it did; I didn't mean it to. He looked stricken.

"I thought I looked smashing!" Bob asserted.

"Well . . ." I faltered. "The shirt goes with the slacks, and the vest goes with the slacks, but . . . well, I don't think the shirt goes with the vest." But I tried to reassure him. It wasn't bad (in fact, it looked quite good once I got used to it).

"Almost every time I get dressed up, you tell me something is wrong! I always tell you when you look nice. Ninety percent of the time you do look nice—you look beautiful—but you won't believe me."

He put on his hat and jacket, picked up his lunch, smiled half-heartedly and left the house. I returned to the stove. The door slammed. He was back, on his way downstairs. "What?" I called. "Did you forget something?"

"I can't go yet. I'm scared," he admitted.

I tried to console him, tried to listen. "Scared of driving? I'll take you."

"No."

"Scared of the people at the meeting?"

"Oh, no . . ."

"Scared of how you look?" I asked finally.

"It's silly . . . not important . . . who cares? Especially in that group!"

"Right!" I exclaimed.

"It shouldn't matter what you think . . . shouldn't matter . . . I used to be so cocky."

I remember when he would talk back to me, tell me that he had his own style, that he would make his own unique fashion statement, thank you. Sometimes I forget I can't talk about the way he looks or acts as once I did. He feels attacked.

"I'm sorry!" I said.

"I know . . . I know . . . I'll be all right. I just can't go yet."

"Let's take a walk then," I suggested. The day was lovely, golden, warm, and much too nice to stay inside anyway.

"Remember what's-her-name [a friend in St. Paul who had Alzheimer's]? She used to look so nice until the end. And then she didn't anymore."

"I won't let that happen to you," I promised. "I'll keep you clean and won't let you go out looking badly." (Can I keep that promise? Even now, he forgets to shave; sometimes he wears wrinkled or spotted clothes.)

"I don't want to be dependent on you! And yet I do want you to help me."

I assured him that he must take care of himself for as long as he can. I assured him that he cares for me, too, by telling me how I look—even if I don't like it sometimes.

There are so many changes, so many established patterns to shift, that we are hardly aware of them all. We discover what they are in the living of them, as we step on one another's toes. We take turns leading now, we make mistakes, we may even hear different music. But the important thing is that we are partners. We still dance.

We made a circle of our driveway. I walked with Bob to the garage; he kissed me and got in the car.

I waved and said, "Have a good time!" He touched the brim of the hat that didn't go with the coat that didn't go with the slacks. Then, smiling a jaunty smile, he waved back.

SEPTEMBER 14

I should be grateful for what I have, not focused on what I don't have, but sometimes I just can't be.

When you see Alzheimer's patients they are sad, sometimes they cry . . . it's because so many things are gone—things they could count on, things they could do. So many dreams. And they know, somehow they know.

It seems like such a waste to learn all these things and gradually lose them! Everybody dies—but most people only die once. I would rather lose my physical ability. If it wasn't my mind . . . If it was anything else.

People with Alzheimer's disease have to learn to be grateful for what they have—not sad or resentful about what they are missing. We have to concentrate on what we can do. But what happens when we can't do anything?

SEPTEMBER 16

I would rather think of myself as a writer, a cook, a gardener, as almost anything but a plumber. Yet there I was, sitting cross-legged on our cold tile floor, staring up at the drinking water faucet on our sink with rapt attention.

If it dripped, I would know that I had accomplished a minor miracle. I had just changed an activated carbon filter, a sediment carbon filter, and an inline activated carbon post filter. If I did it right, the dispenser faucet would begin to drip and then I could, in the following order, open the self-piercing saddle valve, close the dispenser faucet, and open the holding tank valve. Whew! In three short hours, we would have purified drinking water.

I always understood that plumbing was not my vocation. I do not like reading diagrams or memorizing foreign-sounding words to decipher the innards of our water system. Why can't all those pipes just hold water and gurgle and flush themselves . . . and do it for our lifetime?

I was stiff, sitting there on the floor. Nothing dripped from the faucet. Gone was the momentary pride I felt in my accomplishment of completing a new, distasteful task. I get so easily discouraged! Will I ever be able to manage all these household chores? For twenty-five years I have depended on Bob to do them.

He came upstairs and asked, "What's for lunch?"

I explained my predicament. Bob has always been handy and mechanical, willing and able to work his way through our "to do" list. Now he couldn't see the knobs and the dials, couldn't understand the workings of our system. My garbled descriptions didn't help, so we both felt badly.

We knelt in front of the sink. I showed him the saddle valve. "I think it's open, but I don't know for sure if I turned it on or all the way off." I crawled in under the pipe, pointing over my head. "How in the world do you know if you're turning clockwise when it's in this position?"

Before I finished the question, Bob's arm darted under the sink. He fumbled for the knob, turned it, and we heard water gurgle in the pipe. Bob gestured, turning his hand to the right.

"Clockwise is always clockwise," Bob said. "But you did all the rest of it—good job!"

We stood in the middle of the kitchen, watching the lovely, slow succession of drops from the dispenser faucet. Bob put his arm around my wet and dirty shoulder.

"I guess I can be your cheerleader now. We're a good team, aren't we?"

SEPTEMBER 18

A good caregiver is like a good teacher. Unless you listen to your student and understand where the person is coming from, you can't help. You can't make the same assignment for everybody and expect them all to do it.

Think of a classroom of young children. They all have different perceptions of the same thing. It's not like one is false and one is true. They are just different. The teacher has to take that into account. You have to be able to come at people in different ways . . . understand where they are and how they learn. I want people to listen. That means looking for non-verbal clues too, like sadness, or loss of appetite, or emotional outbursts.

I learned a lot from my sister, Leona, who works with children with learning disabilities. She keeps listening, but then she insists on the students doing what they can do, one step at a time, breaking the work into little pieces. She is always enthusiastic. She has taught children to read who didn't believe they could do it!

SEPTEMBER 20

They stood in the driveway—the older man scuffing gravel with his boot, the young man squinting into the sun to look at him. They nodded. There was a hearty handshake; then it was done. The woodworking equipment that Bob bought all those years ago, that he never fully assembled, went to Michael. And many of Bob's dreams went with it.

Michael is a very talented woodworker who built our cabinets and bookcases. Now he is going into business for himself. He needs a workspace and our barn will suit him at least until winter comes. His goal is to cooperate with other craftsmen, sharing jobs and equipment if necessary, so all of them can succeed in this community.

"Amazing!" Michael said when Bob offered to give him the equipment. "It's very expensive!"

"I know," Bob replied.

The payment Bob asked was that Michael be available to help us, especially to help me, when I do not know how to do a complicated household task.

"We want to stay in our house as long as possible," Bob told Michael.

Michael is glad to be called. "Amazing!" he said again. "I'm certainly glad that we ran into you at the concert the other night."

"Oh, no!" I corrected him. "Bob didn't get this idea that night. He has been thinking about it for a long time."

Bob nodded and said. "If you knew me better, you would know I never do anything in a hurry."

"Hmmm . . . " Michael shook his head, then slowly turned to go. Bob and I walked up to the house.

I remember, when my father died, how important it was to my mother that she give his things to people who would really appreciate them. She took a long time deciding who should have his watch, his books, his tools. But the gift that pleased her most, I think, was when she presented Dad's custom-made, matched set of golf clubs to his favorite caddy. I remember still the look on that young man's face. The surprise, the tears, the sheer open-mouthed joy he felt as he stroked the smooth brown leather bag.

We got to the front door and turned to look back. Michael was sitting in his truck . . . just sitting there, staring straight ahead and smiling. He sat for several minutes before he roused himself to start the engine and wave good-bye. Bob beamed and waved back. He had been blessed by the open, uncomplicated acceptance of a freely-offered gift.

It is a mystery, isn't it? Because God first loved us, because we have had the experience of other people giving to us, we are able to give to others. We can give, and take joy in giving, because we have received.

OCTOBER 12

Maybe Alzheimer's patients are like human barometers, sensitive like babies. When there is a change in the family, their reaction is to cry. I don't cry because I'm sad. It's because I'm not clever or creative anymore. I don't know what I want or how I feel, but I sense how you feel. I know when you're busy and when you're anxious.

Maybe Alzheimer's patients *are* barometers. I can't get away with a thing! Bob knows how I am feeling even before I do. I have to monitor my emotions carefully and clarify them for us both. When I get anxious (or when I need to vent), I must try to find a time, a place, another person, a journal . . . some manner in which I can talk without disturbing him.

I can't stand it if you get angry. I'm afraid you'll go away. But I'm much less apt to be upset now than I was before. I used to be so scared when you would go somewhere. Now you tell me where you are going, tell me the times, when you will be back . . . When we can talk it out, I get more rational. Give me a picture of what you are doing so I will know you are coming back.

OCTOBER 20

The tourist season is coming to an end. The atmosphere in town is more relaxed, there are parking spaces available and local people greet each other like long-lost friends. And they are, having been "lost" in the flurry of hosting, and guiding, and entertaining that begins in May and ends when the last leaves fall. We may criticize tourism, but we welcome it, too. Our county needs the business and local residents need the stimulation. If it seems too much of a good thing sometimes, we remember the long winters. All in all, there is a good balance here, an ebb and flow to the year that we can appreciate and complain about at the same time.

Bob likes the quiet season. He wants to spend most of his time at home. He says he doesn't need much company. But this summer he has flourished. We hosted his family, two seminary classmates, and many other friends who were passing through, on a trip to Canada or the Boundary Waters. Some of them stayed in our house, but most did not because our guest room is small, and we have to share a bath. Also because Bob needs a quiet space of his own and time out in his den every day.

Bob's son, Les, said Dad was "perky." Bob's brother could hardly believe he has Alzheimer's, even though he watched their sister succumb to the disease. "He's doing so well! Are you sure about the diagnosis?"

Other visitors, too, said Bob seemed like his old familiar self. They shared memories and gave him the greatest gift of all, recreating his past. In many, many ways, by their presence and in their stories, they told Bob what he means to them. They laughed and teased and lightened the atmosphere in our house. Bob needed this stimulation more than either of us knew. He was tired by it, of course, sometimes too tired. No one else sees the effort it takes him to keep up with others. No one sees the let-down when he is alone.

This week is gray and drizzly dark. Bob spends the days in his den, napping in his chair, listening to public radio or watching TV. At mealtime, he hovers around me in the kitchen and snacks like a bear going into hibernation.

There is a thin line between having too much activity and too little. The line will be constantly moving, surprising us, and we will have to shift to keep our balance. Ebb and flow. Work and rest. Time together and time apart. "For everything there is a season," the preacher says. "A time to break down, and a time to build up; a time to weep, and a time to laugh . . ." (Ecclesiastes 3:1-7).

OCTOBER 24

Bob was excited this morning, looking forward to the day. He was up before the alarm went off, dressing with care. He even reminded me to pack his lunch. Thank you, Barry, for asking Bob to drive with you to a clergy meeting in Duluth!

Our doctor says it's good for Bob to have time away from me and, since most health care professionals are women, it is particularly good for him to have some "guy time."

And it is good for me to have time to myself. I feel giddy! How long has it been? I can't remember the last time I had a whole day at home alone. It has been over a year, certainly . . . Maybe since the diagnosis.

I think back to the years when I was a stay-at-home mom. I wish I could have saved a few of the quiet hours I had to myself when the children were in school. I would withdraw them now, in this future I could not have imagined.

Today I can eat whatever I want; I can wear my old clothes, nap if I'm tired, work at the desk without a single interruption, talk on the phone without being overheard, walk the dogs whenever I need a break. For one whole day, for at least eight hours, I am responsible for no one but myself.

NOVEMBER 1

Once while Lila was visiting she asked, "You two get along well, don't you? You talk things over." We looked at each other, puzzled, then smiled as if to say, "Doesn't everyone?"

Both of us have been divorced. We know the answer to that question. In many, many cases the symbiotic relationship between patient and caregiver will be more strained than it is in ours. We are lucky.

Nonetheless, it is important for each of us to have time alone, some time at home and time away from the house.

We need a change of scenery, a change of company—or maybe no company at all. I take time out occasionally to do errands, go to a meeting, or have lunch with a friend. But only for a few hours once or twice a week, no more.

You know why I get anxious when you're gone? I feel so responsible! What if someone comes to the door? What if the phone rings? When you come back I can relax.

Bob needs time out, too. He is dependent on others to call him and suggest an outing because it is difficult for him to take the initiative, but he is very appreciative when they do.

We spend most of our time at home; we are together almost all day every day. Bob and I are truly blessed that we enjoy each other's company.

AUTUMN SABBATH

Put on your old wool hat, my love.
Come—
let's walk uphill
where noon sun warms our shoulders and
summer ripeness lingers on the breeze.

Drink deep with me the burgundy of oak,
sniff musk bouquet of birch Chablis,
then let us dip and swirl 'til we are dizzy,
do-si-do with muffled steps on careless leaves.

Forget neat piles that we have yet to rake,
the wood to stack, windows to be washed.
Let's be grasshoppers today
and ants, perhaps, tomorrow.

We'll let the dogs run free on rocky ground;
we'll hear the birds call, watch them feed
and toast to their long journey
though they'll pack the sun away.

Put on your hiking boots, a jacket;
I'll bring bread.
Let me take your work-rough hand in mine.
Stay out with me
until the sun goes down.

—Anne Simpson

CHAPTER TWELVE

THE BREAKTHROUGH

When Gail came back for a visit this summer, Bob's young colleague had a conversation with her mentor that was so important I transcribed it for the book:

The Rev. L. Gail Irwin: How did you feel called into the ministry?

Bob: I can remember in high school and at Hamline how I had to fill out all these blanks. They asked us to choose what three occupations we might want to pursue. I put: minister, forest ranger . . . I can't remember the third.

But at Hamline I had a good advisor and he certainly had a big influence on my deciding to go into ministry. I was always grateful, it was the right vocation for me.

Gail: What theological insights have you gained from living with Alzheimer's?

Bob: I came back home from being diagnosed and, at first, I was hesitant about saying anything to anybody, not because I was trying to hide it, but because I realized I needed to take a little time. I did tell our minister and asked him not to say anything, but he announced it from the pulpit the next Sunday morning when I wasn't there. It worked out in the long run, but I was hurt by it. I wanted to avoid being dramatic, and he played to that.

There was a period when I was thinking very hard about it and trying to assimilate it and feeling at death's doorstep, feeling this is the end. A sense of distance—there wasn't much left. Life was short, running out. I was feeling separated from other people, feeling I'm not going to be here long.

But my thinking moved more toward, "Well, I always knew I was going to die, there is an end somewhere and we never know when." There was a growing feeling of trust and a sense of God's presence. Basically, that held.

Gail: How did that feeling come about, do you think? Was it grace?

Bob: Hmmm . . . Yes. We went to a Good Friday service at the Lutheran church, and Pastor John talked about changes in his own life, a time of sadness and loss. He said that our whole community was acquainted with Good Friday grief, and what I began to be aware of was that there really is something about it being good.

We talk about the resurrection, but the Good Friday experience means that God is there not just in the triumph, in the end, but in the process, and there is nothing we can do that Jesus is not with us. He is there in the suffering as well as in the good times . . .

Gail: Possibly more.

Bob: There is just not any place that we can go, anything we can do that he is not there. That was my healing. I realized I was not alone. I had been feeling separated; I felt alone. I believe we are all called to die ourselves that we may be reborn in Christ.

That was my break-through. I never preached about that. About how "good" Good Friday is. That is what makes it holy. We are not alone. I guess this is a personal theology. But I don't think it is a new insight—I just see it now in a new and different way. Existentially, it has a lot more meaning. Not new understanding, but new depth. The Christian faith seems less academic to me now, more personal.

Gail: You mean that Jesus does not bring absence of pain, but he brings the presence of love. . . ?

Bob: Right. In Scripture, God is always with the people when they think it least possible. They see God in their distress when they look back on it in humility. Humility is essential.

Gail: What are you learning about yourself from having Alzheimer's?

Bob: One of the things I feel about Alzheimer's is that the person makes a whole circle. You're born as a baby, and people are excited. They see you as having value, but you can't do anything. The value lies not just in what the child is, but in the potential—what lies ahead.

In Alzheimer's, you come back to being very childlike, like an infant in your ability to function. But value lies not in what you can do, but in your being. People are valuable for what they are in the present, not just for their pasts or for their future potential.

We need to see the person with disease as being a complete person in the moment, not as being a partial person. That was the fallacy in Hitler's Nazism—seeing value only in the superman and disposing of all the others. It ended up destroying the culture.

I have, from the inside, a feeling of reaffirmation of the worth all people have intrinsically, not just for themselves, but for the whole society. If we turn our backs to part of society, we hurt the whole. If we can value elderly people, we will feel better about ourselves as we age. That's a lesson Alzheimer's patients can teach.

There are an awful lot of people who have this disease, or think they do and hide it, and I think it is hard on them. It is hard on society, too, because people are afraid of it. The more we speak about it and see it, the more we will realize that it is not the end . . . I see that better now.

I'm less anxious than before I had Alzheimer's. I'm probably more relaxed than I have ever been. I don't know if that's because there is a dulling in my head. I'm grateful for the energy I once had, to get things done. Now I don't have to get things done so I'm more relaxed.

At the same time, I get tired. But there is a positive to this. I may get angry, but the anger doesn't stay with me like it used to.

Gail: We are all looking for somebody like you that we can just be with. Then we feel free. We don't have to do anything. We, too, can just be and be our selves. You are a very positive type of person to be around in ministry. Yours is a ministry of presence.

Bob: There are times I see colors—I've never read about this—but often in my room I will see red, and it is very comforting. I see it as a sign—and then it is gone. Or I take a shower and all the drops are blue, beautiful blue, and warm—and it is a reminder.

Gail: My experience of you has been that you always seem to have a positive spin. Like when I made some horrendous mistakes during our first year working together, and you would sit me down and say, "Well, it probably had to turn out that way because . . ." You'd find some positive outcome that I couldn't see. It's always been my private joke about you. We could have a nuclear holocaust and you would say, "Well . . . there is probably some benefit to the environment."

Do you see yourself that way? Is that just my perception? You can see the good in Good Friday!

Bob: I do believe I think theologically. That means thinking in a positive fashion, if you keep working at it, because the *theo-* means that you are always trying to find the meaning in things. I look for God in the midst of things and at that point where I find meaning, I find God.

Good humor is a part of the Christian faith because it keeps you from making idols out of all your beliefs. I certainly believe evil is real, but we give it power by making it the absolute reality. Turning everything into black and white, absolutes, is a way of making idols. People can become so sure of themselves, so self-righteous that it becomes their religion. Sometimes the "upside-downness" of the Word is true as well. Like the very idea that Good Friday is good. Both are okay—both the joy and the pain. I really feel that God laughs.

CHAPTER THIRTEEN
LIVING THE QUESTIONS

NOVEMBER 1

"What's our schedule today?" Bob sometimes asks me three or four times before breakfast. If I write it down for him, he can't read my writing. When he writes it down himself, he loses his notebook. If I feel even the slightest degree of irritation, Bob can pick it up right away. He withdraws or becomes defensive. He is right, of course. He can't help not remembering—no amount of effort or discipline can improve his memory.

I am the one who must become self-disciplined. I must learn to quietly tell him, over and over, the same answer to the same questions. And I must learn to exercise the weakest muscle in my psychological anatomy. Grant me patience, Lord . . . and hurry!

NOVEMBER 6

I keep having this recurring dream: we're separated, and we don't have a chance to say goodbye.

Both of us know that we may have to make a decision about a nursing home someday. Bob's sister was able to stay at home until she died, but her husband was able to do things for Eloise that I cannot do for Bob: lift her, turn her, and carry her, for instance. Still, I want us to live together until the end if we possibly can. We are investigating housing options and dreaming about alternatives.

I'm glad we can talk about these things. I want you to know, when I get to the point where I can't help you, I won't feel bad if you put me in a home. I don't want you to resent me, don't want to be a burden. I'll know if you feel that way! I want you to remember me well.

I want to stay home as long as possible. In the nursing home there are too many people. It's too noisy, too crowded. I want a quiet place, a room by myself. I don't want to put pressure on you. But I want to stay with you. I don't want to go away to a home or anything. It would be the end.

My emotions are mixed, too. I know that I will do everything I can to care for Bob myself. I will use respite care and health services, anything—everything—the community offers.

We have seen nursing homes with dementia wings and Alzheimer's units, some of them very hospitable and comfortable, geared for the needs of this special population with well-trained staff. The time might come when I have to admit that Bob would have better care in such a place than I could provide for him.

I think that any decision I make will have the backing of his family; that will be very important. But, no matter what they say, I will feel that I have let him down. Always I may feel as Anne Lamott expresses in *Bird by Bird*:

> The moment I walk in and smell those old people again, and find them parked in the hallways like so many cars abandoned by the side of the road, I start begging God not to let me end up like this. But God is not a short-order cook and these people were once my age. I bet they used to beg God not to let them end up as they have. (81)

DECEMBER 1

If I think about what I can't do, I lose energy. I only seem to have one track left. It's like this morning—I was getting my cereal. You asked me a question. Then everything left my mind! I couldn't answer you. I couldn't remember what I was doing before you talked to me. I was so confused, my mind turned gray. Then I saw the bowl in my hand, so I remembered. Eventually, I got my breakfast. Afterward we could talk.

Other people can do many things at once or be in a place where a lot of different things are happening. But I can't. If there is more than one conversation, if people interrupt, if there is background noise or too much movement . . . I just can't follow. I blank out. I get so tired! It can happen when I am alone, too.

There are lots of books on helping children grow up. What do you do to help people grow down? I feel like I am back at adolescence. I have to break every task into little bits . . . do each thing as I think of it so it doesn't go away. I have to trim all the fat off living.

Wood-chopping is good. Very good! I have to keep my mind on one thing. I like the challenge. It is worthwhile. There is no motor, nothing to worry about. It's good exercise. I need to get exercise! It makes me feel better.

DECEMBER 3

The *Alzheimer's Association National Newsletter* (Winter 1996) describes a research project on functional decline in Alzheimer's disease and functional development in early childhood:

> The correlation suggests that Alzheimer's disease sets into motion a reversal of the abilities humans acquire during early childhood. The care needs in the middle stages are often similar to those of a young child. Using these findings, researchers hope to learn more about how to care for individuals with Alzheimer's disease by further investigating functional losses and studying how abilities are acquired in young children.

When I was a little kid, no one took me seriously. They patronized me, and I knew they were just being friendly or they were teasing. Then, part of getting older was having an adult take me seriously. I remember that if I had information or could do something that could really help, even for just a moment, it was such a wonderful feeling!

DECEMBER 12

Bob tells Pastor John: "I feel like a child."

"Do you have any of the wonder of a child?"

"Maybe . . . I rejoice in doing little jobs. I like being with my family and friends," Bob replies. "I believe there is a purpose in this, but I don't know what it is. Maybe 'a little child shall lead them.' Unless you become like a child with humility, simplicity, dependence, you can't know or show others heaven. I don't have any answers—just so many questions! But a bird does not sing because it has an answer—it sings because it has a song."

"How are your spirits?"

"They're fine."

"Really fine?" Pastor John probes.

"As long as I stay in the present they are. I have good days now. If I think about the past, I get sad. If I think about the future, I'm scared. I only have the present. Today is the only day I have to live.

"At first, I just concentrated on dying. But then I realized that we all know, intellectually at least, that we will die. I knew that before and still I concentrated on living. I can learn to do that now. Otherwise, I feel like I am in a jail with a life sentence.

"Our meaning is given to us," Bob continues. "We run all through life trying to find it, but it is a gift. All meaning-givers, except God's love, go down the drain. Learn to trust every moment, every day. God has been there before you.

"I'm not angry at God. I believe God is here, somewhere. There is a purpose. I am beholden to find it. This may go on for ten to twenty years. My reality will get very distorted. Still, this is reality."

"I had a wonderful lunch with Bob," John told me later. "*He* ministered to me. He has such amazing insights in spite of his disease. He describes the way all of us should live!"

DECEMBER 17

You know how it is when you push and push yourself to do something and you just can't do it any more, so finally you give up? It's easier! It frees you up to do what you can do without beating yourself. Life is easier for me now than it was before I knew that I had Alzheimer's.

It is easier for me, too. Bob knows what he can do, and I know what I must do. I will learn helping skills and he will learn the art of letting go. As our journey continues, we have a map to follow.

Of course, there will be times that we get lost or stumble under the weight of the new burdens that we carry. There will be days so dark that we can't see the path. But we will trudge on. Looking down at the rocks beneath our feet, looking up at the clear or stormy sky with the pillar of cloud and the pillar of fire, we will tread our way.

DECEMBER 19

We all know the commandment from Galatians 6:2 to "bear one another's burdens." Sometimes we don't like it much—most of us feel that our own cares are burden enough. But we all need something to take us out of ourselves. It is a new understanding for Bob and me: If we aren't willing to give up a burden, there is nothing for others to bear. So our burdens can be our gifts. In Charles Williams' book *Descent Into Hell*, the character Stanhope explains this insight to a stubborn friend:

> If you insist on making a universe for yourself, . . . if you want to disobey and refuse the laws that are common to us all, if you want to live in pride and division and anger, you can. But if you want to be part of the

best of us, and live and laugh and be ashamed with us, then you must be content to be helped. You must give your burden up to someone else, and you must carry someone else's burden. I haven't made the universe and it isn't my fault. But I am sure that this is a law of the universe, and not to give up your parcel is as much to rebel as not to carry another's. (99)

DECEMBER 21

You are really interested in what is happening now; you take me seriously; you want to understand, even if you don't always do what I want. If I say I am tired, you believe me. I go lie down, and then I can get going again.

What I appreciate is that you try to understand. Sometimes you interpret for me what I am feeling but can't put into words. That makes me feel very good! You're so helpful—you will play the game with me to help remember someone's name.

DECEMBER 29

"You know what?" the eight-year-old boy who lives next door asked me once.

"No, what?" I responded.

"Mom told me something very sad."

"What was that?" I asked.

"She said someday Bob will even forget how to walk. We all hope he will die before then."

Our neighbor is a compassionate young woman. She cares deeply for Bob. She does not want him to suffer. She is also practical. There are only so many resources to go around—emotional, physical, social, financial resources should not be wasted on the elderly.

I'm sure I felt exactly as our neighbor does when I was her age. But I am not so sanguine now! What I have learned in the past thirty years, what she can't know yet, is that the old can cling fiercely to life. Even when they are very sick, they may hang on to that precious gift—enjoying, sharing, or railing against it—squeezing the last nourishing drops from their portion.

Who are we to decide it is time for them to let go? As the mind and body fall away, it is possible that the flame within burns bright and clean. If we dismiss the disabled persons in our midst, we may hurt ourselves as much as we harm them. We may lose opportunities to be warmed and enlightened.

DECEMBER 30

Bob asked his sons what advice they would have for others whose parents have the disease.

"Be open and accepting," the boys stated. "And be prepared for change. It is going to affect everybody! Don't take your family for granted."

What follows is an excerpt from "Thine Is the Power, but What about Mom?" by the Rev. Jill Geoffrion dedicated to her mother-in-law, a victim of Alzheimer's:

> I often wonder how to react to things Mom says and does.
> My natural inclination is to pretend I didn't hear or notice,
> to look away,
> or just to smile placidly
> while I try to think of something to say
> that might make sense.
> In other words,
> my first reaction is to distance myself
> from the pain that Mom and all of us are feeling.
> I am so grateful for the times I remember
> to look her in the eyes and to connect with her
> in this simple but profound way.
> Why is it so easy to forget
> that she doesn't need me to agree with her,
> or understand everything,
> but that she longs for someone
> to value her enough to look right at her?
> What are we so afraid of seeing?

The temptation to look away
or get away
looms large when I feel confused, embarrassed or fed up.
But I've noticed that when my eyes meet Mom's,
she seems to relax.
What a simple gift of immense value. (185-192)

JANUARY 23

I still have the idea! I think it through until it's clear. But when I try to express it, the words don't come out right. They escape. I worry so much about using the right words and saying it right that I forget what I was trying to say.

I had an idea just now that I wanted to share with you . . . but I got distracted and can't get the idea back. It's like someone erased the blackboard before I had a chance to write it all down. I remember in third grade the teacher wrote on the blackboard, "A mind is a terrible thing to waste."

JANUARY 25

Isn't it funny? When you are young, you know about death and still you think everything will be more or less the same . . . Now I think about death all the time—and endings. I'm kind of separating myself from people, things. It's not sad, really, and I still can't imagine myself not existing, but I feel removed . . . Life will go on without me.

Sometimes I wonder what is real, what has been or what will be. It's so hard to perceive not being here. All the things I've learned, done, and felt—all gone! Where did they go?

FEBRUARY 8

Even over a few months, I can be aware of what I have lost. But I wonder why? Why do some things go and not others? It's interesting! I'm an experiment, like a rat in a maze. Watch me run around. . . .

FEBRUARY 13

Sometimes I think of all the negatives—all the things I did wrong, all the things I didn't do. But the trouble is I don't even know what's real. I don't know what I am remembering. I don't know what's true any more. Sometimes I feel as if I shouldn't have wasted so much time. But if I had it to do over, I don't know if it would be much different. I might not make the same mistakes, but I'd make different ones.

MAY 1

We went to Hawaii. It was as good a trip as Bob dreamed. On a plaque at the Kalaupapa Lookout overlooking the leper colony on the island of Molokai, Bob found these words:

> The social stigma of leprosy has caused untold and needless pain. Many patients have been rejected and forgotten, even by family and friends—as if the disease had erased their humanity.

The history of humanity is much influenced by the frightening diseases of humanity. But it is also true that the more we understand a disease, the less power it has over us.

Modern medicine has done so much to help relieve the fear of so many diseases, but for some reason Alzheimer's is still a "plague" in our society. It has the power and effect of ancient leprosy. Victims feel they must try to hide any symptoms of the disease for as long as they can.

> When Jesus saw a leper, He became a leper. He did not, of course, develop the symptoms. But which is the worst part of the disease, the physical symptoms or the psychological syndrome...? The latter is worse: the loneliness, the mental anguish, the sense of being an outcast. Jesus did not sympathize merely. Certainly he did not patronize. Nor did he bend down in pity, as one who says, "Yes, I know what he feels." He felt it all. He identified Himself with all the horror of it until He could get His shoulder under the burden and lift and dispel it forever. (Leslie Weatherhead, *Salute to a Sufferer*, 61)

One day we talked to a wise Hawaiian elder who told us:

> "In our culture you are not a part of nature, you are all of nature. When you feel big and important, look down between your toes; you are the smallest ant. When you feel small and discouraged, look up and see the endless sky. Everything is a circle unto the end. Everything is a lesson to be learned. 'Aloha' means to breathe with the breath of life."

On the last day of our trip, as we walked on the beach and whispered goodbye to the islands, I wrote Bob a poem:

ALOHA
I am the rumbling earth
I am the blue-green waves
and the white surf
crashing on the sand.

I am the golden beach,
the footprints on the beach,
the foam that erases the footprints,
the sandpiper that chases the foam.

I am the lava rocks,
sharp and rough and black.
I am the memories,
jagged and broken.

I am the Spirit
that washes your soul
that smoothes your past,
that oozes between crevices in your mind.

I am the pain that ebbs,
the laughter that flows –
onto the rocks
into the rain
into the tears
back to the sea.
I am forever.

—Anne Simpson

CHAPTER FOURTEEN
GUIDE FOR CAREGIVERS

Maybe it is lucky for humankind that Moses didn't write on a disk. If we had to carve our guidelines for caregivers on stone tablets and tote them down a mountain, you can be sure that we would have no more than ten.

But, since space and weight are not considerations for us, we will try to share whatever we have learned so far on our journey through this wilderness called Alzheimer's disease.

These are not commandments, they are suggestions. They are not ranked in order because all of them are important. Each patient is different and each caregiving relationship unique, but there are universal needs and we hope that this guide will be helpful in most situations.

BOB'S GUIDE

INCLUDE ME

In my mind, one of the most important things you could do for me to make me feel comfortable in a group of people is to include me. Not so much by asking questions unless you are willing to help me answer them (which I would appreciate), but by including me in your smiles and eye contact.

I have always enjoyed being part of small groups. But now I feel sad in a group of three or more. Part of it is my fault. I can easily fall into self-pity and have strong feelings that no one really wants to be with me because I'm limited and I can't remember or get the right word. Sometimes I can't get the words or, in some instances, my reactions are inappropriate. But I hope you will include me.

Often when I am in a group I feel that I am invisible—or that people are trying to avoid looking at me. Eye contact is important, but if I sit for awhile and all the eye contact is to everyone but me, it brings feelings that I don't belong or that I'm invisible. It would mean a lot if you would include me in your eye contact and your smiles as much as you do others in the group. Caregivers could help by making sure they have eye contact with the patient, setting an example for the whole group.

I don't have as much to contribute to the conversation, but I love being equally included. "In as much as you have done it to the least of these," you will be blessed.

TALK TO ME

I wish people would talk to me directly, as they always used to do. I try to talk directly to them, but now I feel that they are more apt to talk about me, talk over my head. Where do they think I am?

When I was starting my ministry, I was a little in awe of older people, a little scared if they were sick. Now I want to tell others: there is almost nothing you can say that will bother me—you can't say a "wrong" thing. What pains me is when you stay away or say nothing at all.

You can talk about the weather, tell me what you've been doing. Did you see anyone I know? Tell me a joke—I might get it. Ask my advice—I am glad to give it. Ask me simple yes-or-no questions. I especially like to talk about the "good old days" and memories we share. If I don't understand, you will know it. Try, try again. I will appreciate your effort.

DO NOT TRY TO BE MANIPULATIVE

A few years ago we went to a video presentation on Alzheimer's for health care professionals. The video was made at a large national conference, and it was presented here, at our clinic, in three parts. The speaker was a good public speaker. She spoke for an hour and a half each presentation. She balanced serious topics with humor in a way that kept the audience's attention.

The topic was, as I understand it, how healthy caregivers could and should use their imagination to trick Alzheimer's patients into doing what the professionals wanted them to do without using force. The speaker's message was that professionals need to be more clever than patients, and it's okay to tell lies, make up stories, do anything to trick the patient.

This attitude reminded me of an incident that occurred when I was minister at Macalester-Plymouth church in St. Paul. A very precocious four-year-old son of two teachers at the college showed me how he was training a stray cat to do what it wanted to do. "What does *it* want to do?" I asked him. "Why, it wants to wait till church is over and then go home with me!" he replied.

I believe there is a more honest and better way. When I went to the video class, I believe there was a different dynamic than there would have been otherwise. When a person has something that is debilitating, others get uneasy. If everyone in the room is healthy, they can be very certain about what the disabled person wants or needs. But because I had Alzheimer's and I was a real person, they wanted to know what I thought. If I had not been there, they would have critiqued the material in an academic way and then gone home.

But some of the people knew me, and all of them knew I had Alzheimer's. I am still quite articulate, so they didn't just see a patient to be manipulated. They saw a person who still has real feelings and deserves respect. Patients want to be with people who will enjoy them and understand, not with people who just try to outwit them.

LISTEN

I have something to say. Take time to hear me out. I have a hard time finding words sometimes, and there are many things I don't remember, but I can make myself understood.

We still speak the same language. Don't jump to conclusions about what I am saying.

It helps me when people ask me what I am saying, really take time to listen, help me to articulate. If they keep asking "Is it this . . . is it that. . . ?" it can be a real breakthrough. Sometimes I don't know what is really bothering me. When I can finally say it, I relax. I discover things for myself by talking about what is really bothering me. I can sort it out if someone listens. It helps the caregiver to learn, too.

When we have two perceptions of things, it is easy to think that mine is distorted because I have Alzheimer's. There is a tendency to believe other people's impressions of the patient. You speak for us, you tell us what we want or how we feel. But my perceptions of things are as real as those of anyone else. Maybe when there are two perceptions it is just as simple as that—two people seeing something in two different ways. The truth may be somewhere in between.

When I used to visit people in the congregation, many times I would wonder to myself what I was doing there, what was the point of it all—even when I wanted to be there and knew I should be. But sometimes something would break through and a totally different dynamic would happen. I think a factor might have been that I was seriously listening. That changes everything. You have to go deep. You have to shed self-consciousness to be totally with the other person.

TREAT ME AS YOU ALWAYS HAVE

I am not invisible. I am not contagious. Or breakable. Or dangerous. I am the same person. Maybe I am a little different, but I am not just "Bob with Alzheimer's," I am Bob. And I am an adult. Don't treat me like a child.

LET ME HELP

I can give my time, my physical strength, my advice, my friendship. Let me give, in my own way, whatever you want from me. I don't want to be always on the receiving end.

GIVE ME A ROLE

Patients need a role. In the small town where I grew up if an elderly man could no longer farm, the family and community tried to find other ways for him to contribute. People made time for him, he became a social cause . . . But everyone is so busy now.

I remember a boy who was injured in a farm accident when I was young; he couldn't do much, but he liked to go into town with his parents. There was one building he liked to stand and lean against while his parents were shopping; we all knew it was "his corner." If he stood too long, he'd start to slump. So when we went by, we'd push his knees and straighten him up again. Everybody did that. He was part of us.

TELL—DON'T ASK

When you come up to me, especially if we are in a public place, move slowly and speak softly. Introduce yourself. Even if I know you, I may not be able to find your name and then we will both feel badly. Don't ask if I remember you! Let me save face. Say, "Hi, Bob, I'm _____." Then I can say, "Of course you are! I'm glad to see you" (and I will be).

Tell me what you want me to do. I can say yes or no, but I can't make choices. Tell me one thing at a time.

RESPECT MY FEELINGS

I can be very emotional at times. Do not try to talk me out of anger or comfort me in sadness. Please don't take my feelings upon yourself. Just sit with me, if I want you to, or let me have my own quiet space. I have a right to my moods.

RESPECT MY INTUITION

All my feelings are heightened now, and I seem to be more aware of other people's feelings. We have friends who went on a trip to China. I knew something was wrong during their trip. They came back early because one of them was sick.

Maybe my intuition sounds dumb sometimes but, on the other hand, maybe Alzheimer's patients have special insights. Pay attention to them.

ENCOURAGE ME

Have enthusiasm about what I, the patient, can do. Hand-in-hand with this disease goes a sense of worthlessness. If someone makes me feel that I can do something helpful or fun, I feel lively again.

I have a hard time believing that I can do something worthwhile. It's difficult for me to tell myself that I can accomplish something. I might need help to make it happen.

BE POSITIVE

Sometimes I feel inadequate. I've messed up. I'm irritating because I keep forgetting what people have just told me. I'm not able to read any longer, and I can't remember what I just heard.

It is important that people close to the patient say things that are hopeful and upbeat. Like children, we want to be with people who enjoy us for who we are now, who don't just think about what we will be when we grow up—or down.

A child is totally dependent. If parents and others do a good job, the child will grow to independence, and the parents' job will get easier. With Alzheimer's patients, it's just the reverse. The caregiver's job will get harder and harder, but maybe we won't be totally dependent if you will just let us have some control over our lives. People are as valuable at the end of life as they are at the beginning.

ANNE'S GUIDE

In *Out of Solitude*, Henri Nouwen writes:

> The friend who can be silent with us in a moment of despair or confusion, who can stay with us in an hour of grief and bereavement, who can tolerate not knowing, not curing, not healing, and face with us the reality of our powerlessness, that is the friend who cares.

There is no better description of caregiving. Paul states it, too, in Romans 12:15: "Rejoice with those who rejoice, weep with those who weep."

There are more and more people in our society today who have been identified as victims of Alzheimer's disease during the early stages. They look like you and me. They act like people afflicted with any other disease—aware of limitations, learning to live with them, refusing to be defined by illness. Many of these patients exhibited symptoms before age 65, so like Bob, they are labeled "early-onset." They may live with the disease for fifteen or twenty years.

It is vitally important for us to understand and support these men and women and to encourage the families and communities that care for them. Here is a list of suggestions that I have started to add to Bob's. Please add your own, and pass them on.

STUDY

A few years ago I didn't even know how to spell *Alzheimer's*. Since Bob was diagnosed, I have received a great deal of valuable information from a number of sources.

As a first step, I highly recommend contacting the Alzheimer's Association. People at the association have sent packets of information to us, and to each of Bob's sons, free of charge. They have an extensive book list from which we have ordered. There is a nurse to answer questions. The phone staff at both the national headquarters and at our regional office have been unfailingly helpful and polite. You can contact the association at:

The Alzheimer's Association
919 North Michigan Ave.
Suite 1000
Chicago IL 60611-1676
phone: 1-800-272-3900
fax: 1-312-335-1110

Talk to your doctors, social services, and other people who have experience with the disease. Use the Internet. If you're like me, you may need your 10-year-old neighbor to help access it using a computer at your local library, but it's worth the effort. There is a wealth of material out there. Start with <www.alzheimers.org>.

Join a support group if there is one in your area. Some cities have groups for patients in the early stages as well as for caregivers. In this remote area, our county has a Caregivers' Group for people in a variety of situations. We tell our individual stories, we have workshops on topics common to us all: grief, loss, stress, etc. It is a good resource and I have met people whose lives inspire me.

BE OPEN TO A "LEARNING OPPORTUNITY"

Like it or not, I am learning new skills as I take over Bob's household jobs. I am discovering the feeling of freedom that comes from knowing how to do things myself. Like it or not, Bob is learning the freedom that comes from letting go of jobs that have always been his portion.

We are learning new things about each other and about ourselves—who we are and what we need. We are learning about other people from their response to us. We are learning to recognize what makes a friendly environment for diseased persons. We feel powerful when we can teach what we have learned.

We are finding out what it means to live each day by doing one thing at a time. As John Robinson said to the Pilgrims, "There is yet more light to break forth from God's holy Word." We must learn to trust the Word. As Bob encourages patients to speak for themselves, so I would urge caregivers.

SHARE YOUR EXPERIENCE

Write letters. Keep a journal. Talk about it. It will help you to clarify your feelings and maintain objectivity. It may help others to understand this mysterious disease.

PLAN FOR THE FUTURE

Plan wills, health care provisions, maybe a living trust. Your lawyer can help you with these matters and so can Legal Aid, which often gives free advice to families of Alzheimer's patients to prevent spousal impoverishment.

We are trying to simplify our lives on many levels and to save money for future health care costs.

Our doctor says it is wise to have patterns established before they are needed: arrangements for days off or for respite care, safe and convenient housing, nursing services. But Bob does not want to change anything until he has to. Alzheimer's is a long, gradually debilitating disease. We need to provide for emergencies and then let go, relax, and trust the process.

LIVE IN THE PRESENT

This is a balancing act. The experience will be different for every patient and family. It seems like a paradox: save for the future, spend in the present. But sometimes the best investment is in something the patient can enjoy here and now.

Bob had always wanted to go to Hawaii. So we went. We walked the beaches in March instead of plowing snow. Maybe it is reckless to spend money this way, but if we are ever going to travel it has to be now. Thinking about the trip and planning for it gave us both something to look forward to.

HAVE REALISTIC EXPECTATIONS

When I was pregnant with my first child, I thought no little infant could change my grown-up way of doing things. I got here first, didn't I? This baby would just have to fit into my life . . . I thought that about caregiving, too, at first. I was relatively young and healthy. I could just add this job to my daily routine and everything would go on as it had before.

We interrupt your life's program to bring the following message: Your plans will be cancelled, interrupted, changed, turned upside down by Alzheimer's disease. Like parenthood, it will bring blessings and surprises and difficulties that you cannot possibly anticipate. The Alzheimer's patient is like a young child, exploring a new world, afraid of the unknown. Caregivers develop a sixth sense, as parents do, and we live with low-level anxiety: Where is the patient now? What is he doing? What does she need?

This disease will not go away. The patient will not get better. Expect to feel loss and grief. Grief is not something you get over, it's something you work through—time and time again.

Your children may or may not be able to help you; they have busy, independent lives and their own issues to resolve. Friends may or may not keep in touch; many people are afraid of Alzheimer's disease.

Don't count on the patient to help you. He may or may not be able to offer support. Except in the early stages, decisions will be up to you and your advisors. When it is offered, accept help as the gift it is. Find out what services are available in your community. Don't be too proud to use them.

Know that there will be bad days. I have them, and so does Bob. Sometimes they seem to come out of nowhere; other times they are triggered by feeling too much responsibility, facing too many decisions, having too many dead-end conversations. I have to remind myself to walk away, take time out, ask myself if it is really important.

BE GENTLE WITH YOURSELF

Like all caregivers, I want to do this right. I want to be the kind of help to Bob that he deserves. I want to prove to myself that I can be the kind of competent, nurturing, loving, patient woman that I always wanted to be. But I will fail. All caregivers know there are times when we fail. We compare ourselves to others who seem to do it better. We feel guilty when we get impatient or tired or depressed.

Ease up on yourself. You have never done this before. Every Alzheimer's patient is individual, every caregiving relationship unique. Learn from your mistakes. Ask and accept forgiveness. With God's help, you will do the best that you can do.

You won't go to jail if you pay your bills a few days late. Your house and yard don't have to look like Martha Stewart's. Your meals don't have to taste like Julia Child's. Besides, if you serve meatloaf three nights in a row, who but you will notice?

LAUGH

Bob says he has always liked people . . . now he can look forward to meeting new ones every day. He tells his grandchildren that he has an advantage over them: he can hide his own Easter eggs.

Our friend Mary's mom has Alzheimer's. She says, "To me she has always been beautiful. She still is! But my siblings only see the sad and mournful part. They don't visit Mom at all because they are so depressed about it. Frankly, I would rather be with her than them. Mom is funny! She laughs."

If the patient goes off on a tangent, go along . . . You won't be able to get back to the subject for awhile, anyway. If he says it's Wednesday when it's Monday, does it really matter? You'll never win an argument with an Alzheimer's patient. If she forgets the punch line to her story, help create one. Keep communication open.

How we respond to what happens is more important than what is happening to us or to the patient. As Yogi Berra said, "Remember that whatever you do in life, 90 percent is half mental."

SING

Bob sent me a card that is both a reminder and a consolation. I keep it on my desk. It reads: "The woods would be very silent if only those birds sang who sing the best." I thought my role as caregiver would be to sing Bob's song. I was wrong. Bob is singing . . . er, humming . . . his own song. A bit off-key, perhaps. But so it has always been. My job is to listen, to supply lyrics occasionally, to accompany the melody I hear.

We have always shared a deep love and appreciation for music, though neither of us can carry a tune. Together, we make a joyful noise! And we harmonize when I can recognize and accept that we have a common condition—that within my own body, which seems strong and healthy now, there lurks the aging and diseased woman I will become.

WATCH YOUR TONE OF VOICE AND BODY LANGUAGE

Clergy and other counselors are taught the importance of being a non-anxious presence. Bob explains, "Don't get annoyed with me! What good does that do? Don't assume that I don't care or I'm not paying attention when I keep asking you the same thing . . . Just talk around and around a subject till it registers. Keep giving me clues if I don't remember. Start with the farthest back memories and any detail you can think of to make the connection."

When I am impatient, distracted, or in a hurry, Bob knows it immediately. He tunes in on feelings now, not words. He feels anxious when I am anxious, and he feels threatened as well; almost always, he interprets any kind of stress as anger and then he assumes that I am angry at him. Usually, I am not.

I am learning to read Bob's body language as well as my own. We are genetically engineered for flight or fight, so anger comes first to hands and feet. When Bob clasps and unclasps a fist, when he stomps his foot while seated, then I know he is agitated. I can back off for awhile or I can help him tell me what is wrong.

We are body, mind, and spirit. As Bob's mind begins to fail, as he loses his eyesight and his other senses dull, both of us have a new respect for the soothing power of touch and the sacred vocabulary of sex. As babies, our first connection to the world is through the sense of touch; it may be the last sense we lose.

UNDERSTAND THE PATIENT'S EMOTIONAL AGE

Do not think of the patient as being his or her chronological age! There are studies proving that the stages of child development are shifted into reverse by Alzheimer's.

ESTABLISH A SENSE OF ORDER, BOUNDARIES

It is not appropriate for a caregiver to respond in a childish manner to a patient's child-like behavior—though, sometimes, the temptation can be hard to resist! I am reminded of Bob's father, his reaction to an outburst Bob's sister once had. She was a senior in high school and had just gotten her first B after a record of all A's. She was screaming uncontrollably. Their father quietly poured a cup of cold water on her head and shocked her out of the fit. His was a deliberate, adult response. He maintained order; he established his sense of right and wrong. He soothed her (and he made her mop up the mess).

Patients may not need such dramatic actions, but they do need to have their caregivers set definite boundaries. They need a daily routine for meals, activity, sleep, quiet stimulation: classical music instead of rock, one or two people instead of a party, if possible a room of their own. Bob has a den where he can retreat from household activity, smoke his pipe, nap in his recliner, watch TV . . .

The patient has a right to his own moods, to her own feelings—to pain. You are deeply affected by what is happening to your loved one, but you cannot take on the patient's disease. You have your own burdens. Keep them separate.

ENSURE PATIENT SAFETY

Most patients are deeply afraid of being abandoned; many of them shadow their caregivers. "Where are you? What are you doing?" They stroke and pat us to reassure themselves of our presence. Whether at home, in a social setting, or a care facility, patients need to know that they are attended. The environment must be monitored carefully so they cannot get lost and so they cannot harm themselves or others.

DO NOT MAKE ASSUMPTIONS

Do not assume that all health problems are related to Alzheimer's or that all mental and emotional responses are distorted by disease.

DO NOT BLAME THE PATIENT

Blame the disease instead of the patient. Your loved one may have marked changes in personality, depending on what parts of the brain are affected. Bob is still the kind and gentle person that he always has been. We are lucky. Many patients are not—through no fault of their own.

BE FLEXIBLE

When Bob wants to do something, or ask me something, he feels great urgency about doing it now because he is afraid that he will forget about it and that when he remembers it will be too late. Get used to being interrupted! Sometimes, if I simply can't leave what I am doing, I reassure Bob that I will take responsibility for remembering what it is that concerns him. I'll write it down—making sure he sees me do it—and follow up as soon as I am able. If he knows he can trust me, he can relax.

What I do on a given day is determined by how Bob is feeling; I must wrap my day around his. We make plans ahead of time, of course, but they may be cancelled, changed or fine-tuned. When Bob has had too much stimulation, he wants to stay home; when he has had enough company he wants to be alone with me. It has not been easy for me to give up this control of my time or to disappoint others who are counting on me. And sometimes I need to remind myself: plants that are root-bound produce the most blossom.

FIND THINGS TO CELEBRATE

Bob says Alzheimer's patients should be grateful for abilities they still have, not mournful for what they have lost. Compared to what the patient used to do, accomplishments may be small. But for who the person is now, recognize that they may be monumental.

Patients must be encouraged to do anything for themselves that they can. Like parents who hear their toddlers demand, "I'll do it myself," or women in their sixties who receive repeated offers of household help from newly-retired husbands, caregivers must listen to the demands for recognition. We must accept help or advice, support fumbling attempts at independence and affirm every success with, "Good job!"

In *Aging*, Henri Nouwen asks, "Where else do we realize that we are valuable except in the eyes of those who by their care affirm our best self?"(101). Every time we care—deeply care—for another person we will learn about him or her, and we will learn about ourselves. We will grow and change, and we may become more patient and loving people. We will always carry past mistakes with us, and we will make new ones—count on it! They may be different ones than the mistakes we made in other relationships or at other times, but there seems to be no limit to the human ability to improvise.

A young friend who has mental retardation says about her life, "It don't easy." Caregiving "don't easy," either; yet, all of us grow up doing it from the time we are old enough to to mother a doll or tend a puppy. We learn to love and care for our siblings and peers, spouses and children, until someday we may care for our parents. Caregiving is the "golden cord" that connects us, a minister once said.

We need the old, the very young, the infirm, and the dependent to teach compassion, to expand the humanity of those of us who are—temporarily—of strong mind and body. When we see caregiving as the life ministry that it is, we will find it both easier and more satisfying. It is the work we have been doing—and receiving—all along.

PRAY

In 1 Thessalonians 5:14-17, Paul says, "Admonish the idle, encourage the faint-hearted, help the weak, be patient with them all . . . rejoice always, pray constantly."

Prayer can help us through the most difficult times. Thomas Merton offers the following prayer in *Thoughts in Solitude*. It has been an inspiration to me.

> My Lord God, I have no idea where I am going. I do not see the road ahead of me. I cannot know for certain where it will end. Nor do I really know myself, and the fact that I think I am following your will does not mean that I am actually doing so. But I believe the desire to please you does in fact please you. And I hope I have that desire in all that I am doing. I hope I will never do anything apart from that desire. And I know that if I do this you will lead me by the right road, though I may know nothing about it. Therefore, I will trust you always, though I may seem to be lost and in the shadow of death. I will not fear, for you are with me, and you will never leave me to face my perils alone. (83)

REMEMBER THE PATIENT'S STORY

Bob was right all those years ago when he said he had lost his stories. He was more accurate than he could have known. Dr. Steven Miles of the Center for Bioethics in Minneapolis says that a demented person cannot imagine himself in relation to his story: "Dementia marks the mortal end of our ability to play with life's circumstances and to imagine a new kind of story." Bob is squarely in the middle of the final chapters of his life. He vaguely remembers the plot so far, the setting and many of the characters; he has no ability to envision how the story will develop. Every day he writes a new page.

It is hard for a healthy person to imagine such disorientation! In his paper "Imagination and the Care of Demented Persons," Dr. Miles explains:

> Loss of imagination, not memory, is the harbinger of dementia. . . . The loss of imagined possibilities is often only realized in retrospect. It seems so minor, in light of present disabilities and in light of the deterioration that is to follow. But we should recognize the loss of imagination as the cataclysmic blow it is. It disables a person's ability to plan, to share the family's sense of grief and burden. It destroys empathy, the cornerstone of love.

But Dr. Miles offers encouragement, as well as a challenge, to caregivers:

> Though dementia is a loss of storytelling capacity by those who are afflicted, it is not so for those who care for afflicted persons. . . . The care of a demented person is itself a family story in which the demented person still participates as the object of caregiving, as a legend is created and sustained and handed down. It instructs the grandchildren who watch the children care as each moves up the generational ladder. . . . The care of demented persons is a story that we tell ourselves, to each other, and to our children. It is these stories that we should solicit, hearken to, and seek to improve.

EPILOGUE

It is almost four years since this journal began, since we knew that we were entering the wilderness of Alzheimer's disease. When I read some of the early entries, I realize that we have come a long way.

Looking back, I am amazed to discover that I can scarcely remember our life before Alzheimer's. I cannot recapture feelings that I had only four years ago, especially the feelings of being trapped that overwhelmed me when we were adjusting to the diagnosis. Strangely enough, I do not feel as confined now as I did then—though I most certainly am. I have not been away from the house by myself for a whole day in more than three years!

I understand what John Bayley, English critic, professor, and novelist, was saying in an interview with the *New York Times* (Dec. 30, 1998). He described his marriage to Iris Murdoch, celebrated author, shortly before her death from Alzheimer's: "Though I have a very good memory—I can remember where we went and what we did—I can't remember the feel of it, you see, the sensation of a person who was completely normal. It's partly a good thing, because she seems perfectly normal to me at present."

Though Bob may seem so to me, and though he is the same person he has always been, Bob is not perfectly normal, either. The results of his last testing at the Mayo Clinic show marked deterioration. In the short exam for mental status, he could not name the day, the month, the year, his birth date, or the president of the United States. He could not do math sums in his head; he could not repeat, in any order, five words the doctor asked him to remember. When Bob was diagnosed, he scored 31 out of a possible 38. Four years later, he scored 16. "The train is coming down the track," one nurse acknowledged.

We have adapted so far. We have made adjustments that once would have seemed impossible, so the ones ahead of us are less frightening than once they were. In the 1960s we used to say, "Wherever in the world you find yourself . . . there you are." The good news is that, eventually, wherever we find ourselves seems normal.

Bob and I used to have wonderful long conversations—laughing, arguing, analyzing, exploring ideas and emotions. And though I miss the intensity and the excitement of our earlier talks, I can't recapture the feeling of them. Now we talk with a lot of pantomime on Bob's part (he's an accomplished actor, fortunately) and a lot of guessing on mine. We can communicate with this challenging new game—almost as important, we can laugh.

Sometimes I am amused that issues that seemed so big at the beginning of our journey are almost inconsequential now. Bob and I take it for granted these days that I will do the chores, the driving, manage the finances, plan the schedules. Alzheimer's dragged us, kicking and screaming, into new patterns, but they are established, even comfortable. I have taken leadership in a marriage that was an equal partnership for over twenty years; the new balance seems "normal" to us both. So what was the fussing and whining all about?

I remind myself that we have many things to be thankful for. We are surrounded by beauty—by beauty in the wild woods behind our house and the creatures making their homes there; by beauty in the lake's mysterious presence, infusing life on the North Shore; by beauty in the music we hear, and the books I read aloud; by beauty in the friends and family who love us and let us love them.

People in this community have been incredibly kind. Clerks in the stores help Bob if he has trouble counting money, and they never short-change him. Golfers, who once might have been irritated by his slow pace, now help him find the ball and sort his clubs. Repair men and women make house calls to help him maintain machinery and do household tasks. They do so without making him feel embarrassed or put down. Health care professionals, lawyers, bankers, church members, friends . . . "This whole county is a support group," the public health nurse explains. So is our extended family.

Some people avoid us, of course. We expected that. But we have been as surprised by friends who turned away as by those who came forward. Either way, relationships are clearly defined now—no pretenses, no games.

I have established new habits in the last few years. I have "unlearned" the patterns of juggling I acquired as a young mother and domestic engineer (when I could cook supper and talk on the phone at the same time, with a baby on my hip, a toddler at my feet, a load of laundry whirling in the dryer, and a dog whining to go outside). Now I deliberately do one thing at a time; I plan very few activities in a given day, and I expect to be interrupted. Bob is most comfortable when he can keep me in sight, reassured if I am within reach.

Our life seems perfectly normal until I talk to friends who are making independent plans to travel, attend workshops, visit grandchildren, or serve on boards and committees. I know that I did those things, too, once upon a short time ago, but I cannot imagine such freedom now. Sometimes I envy them, but I wouldn't want to trade places.

Many newly retired people wrestle with unexpected pressures: the temptation to be—or seem to be—as busy, productive, important, and successful as they were during their working years. Bob and I don't have those pressures; we are old for our age. In fact, it is awkward for us to spend too much time with healthy contemporaries. I am put in the uncomfortable position of protecting Bob from too much of the very stimulation I may crave, because he can't always keep up with people's conversations or activities. And our friends' lives are so fast-paced that they can't "keep down" with him.

By necessity, our life is more limited and more focused now—but in many ways it is lighter. Our simple schedule sustains and nourishes us. It's like living out of a suitcase and not wasting time deciding what to wear. It's like cooking dinner when the refrigerator is almost empty, but you can't get to the store—sometimes these are the most creative meals. We make do with what we have, and we feast on leftovers.

Living with Alzheimer's disease is creative, too. It is not passive; it is not wasted time. Bob is challenged every day to use the abilities he has left. I am challenged to encourage and affirm his many strengths, to learn new skills that can help us both and teach them to others, to live with questions about our future. We will have many changes ahead.

Someday we will have to move to a smaller, handicapped-accessible house or apartment. But where? Bob will need respite care. Can I keep him at home? Will he always know, at some level, what is happening to him—or will the journey become easier for Bob as it becomes harder for me? (I hope so!)

An experienced caregiver trains novices by warning them, "If you think caregiving is difficult today, just wait . . . It will be worse tomorrow." The only choice, then, is to make the most of today and to hope there is time to adjust to each new loss before tomorrow comes.

The process of watching my beloved husband deteriorate is painful, lonely, and immensely sad. I cannot deny it; I have spells of depression and self-pity. I have days when I am so frustrated that I go into the garage and sit in the car with all the windows rolled up, so I can scream without being overheard. I have times when I am impatient with Bob and feel terribly guilty after I let it show. I can see the losses, the bad side, the half empty glass.

Bob has dark days, too, when he is overcome by grief or feelings of isolation, but he seems genetically engineered to see the glass half full. And his optimistic attitude is more than a personality trait; it is a choice. "I keep trying to be upbeat," he says, "because it seems right." Living gracefully with Alzheimer's is his mission. If I tell him that he is being unrealistic, he retorts, "It's not that I don't see the problems. There is a lot of pain underneath."

A young doctor in our community was killed with her family in a tragic auto accident three years ago. The last entry written in her journal was: "Joy is a decision!" It is Bob's decision. I pray that it can be mine as well. In withdrawing from outside activity, I have decided to draw deeper into myself, and I am discovering the quiet joys of solitude.

It seems to me that if we are lucky enough to live out our allotted span, our lives assume the shape of a cross. When we are young, we reach out to embrace our parents, our peers, and the natural world around us. We stretch and grow horizontally. As we age, the outside world grows smaller. One by one, we are cut off from people and activities that have given us meaning. Now our challenge is to grow vertically—up to God, down into self. It is precisely at the place where the vertical and the horizontal come together, where the arms of the cross meet, that we can find our holy Comforter and Companion for the journey.

Bob and I are coping, as all of us must cope at some time with some handicap, disability or disease. Said Father Joseph who served the Hawaiian leper colony, "One's Molokai can be anywhere."

We are by no means alone in coping with Alzheimer's. It is estimated that one in ten persons over age 65, and half of the population over 85, have some form of dementia! In nursing homes across the country, it affects 60 percent of all patients. In years ahead, research may bring treatments or a cure. Meanwhile, Alzheimer's is a wilderness, part of the mystery of all creation—a part which, like it or not, many of us will have to explore.

I love the words of Ruth Duck's hymn, "Lead on, O Cloud of Yahweh," found in *Everflowing Streams* (Pilgrim Press, 1981). As we travel, I would like to loudly sing the second verse for Bob and other patients:

> Lead on, O fiery pillar,
> We follow yet with fears,
> But we shall come rejoicing,
> Though joy be born of tears.
> We are not lost, though wandering,
> For by your light we come,
> And we are still God's people,
> The journey is our home. (77)

There is a Jewish proverb that holds "if there are two courses of action, try to take the third." When people die after a long and debilitating illness, they are said to have "succumbed" to it or they are praised for valiantly fighting against it. Bob believes there is a third way.

You don't go gentle into the dark night, but you can't rage against it either. You have to face the darkness, eventually, and make your peace with it. That's the third way.

I'm not glad I have Alzheimer's, but I have a good life. I can do things I like, I have work to do . . . it is not all negative. People will never admit they have this disease if all they can see is negative. Patients need to do as much possible, to live their fullest life and to discover joy where it can be found. But we need to speak up for ourselves! There is nothing more important.

"Get a diagnosis," is the first thing I would say to those who suspect they have Alzheimer's. Then tell people. Don't try to hide it. When you feel anxious, share that feeling. Say you have Alzheimer's—people will be helpful. It takes the pressure off of you. I haven't had many bad experiences.

Some people will be bothered, but most will be helpful; they may even be warm toward you. Just say, for instance,

"I have Alzheimer's so I can't remember," or "I can't take too many directions," or "I'm tired now, and I have to rest." You get to know the people you can count on and those who stay away. They are embarrassed. People stay away from Alzheimer's patients if you are not open, because they don't know what to do with you. You get more isolated if you're not honest!

Next, I must say this: some of the best days I have had have been the ones since I knew I had Alzheimer's. We have a good life! Bad days, yes, but now we know what we are dealing with. The worst times were before the diagnosis. I wish people would ask me . . . I might have time to tell them. It doesn't always go fast.

I don't take things for granted any more. I treasure the good times now. On a nice, easy day when we don't have anything planned, I enjoy myself. Little spells in the midst of it, sometimes . . . my emotions take over . . . but then I bounce back. Before the diagnosis, I did some things wrong. I did a lot of dumb things—but it wasn't me who did all of them. It was the disease. And I did a lot of things right, too! Everybody makes mistakes. There's a tendency to blame the victim if you don't know somebody has Alzheimer's.

I'm anxious to talk while I can! There are many things the medical people don't know. They are interested in my story. Maybe I can help others. I remember when we first got back from Rochester. I was crying and feeling bad. Anne came in and said it would be good to write down my feelings. She convinced me that it would be worthwhile. That was a real turn-around. I realized I could do something. I could share what I knew. I wasn't useless; I might help other people. I had insights that only those with Alzheimer's know. It was the beginning of change in my attitude.

I think it is particularly hard for men to talk about their feelings. We usually aren't brought up that way. But I would challenge all patients to share their insights—they will all be different. We must not hide.

When I first got the diagnosis, I felt death on my shoulder. But now—I've never been happier. There are many blessings. It's not over!

People say to me, "You don't look like you have Alzheimer's!" I tell them, "*This* is what Alzheimer's looks like.

BIBLIOGRAPHY

Bayley, John. *Elegy for Iris.* New York: St. Martin's Press, 1999.

Davis, Robert. *My Journey into Alzheimer's Disease.* Wheaton, Ill.: Tyndale House Publishers, 1989.

Duck, Ruth. "Lead on, O Cloud of Yahweh." *Everflowing Streams.* Eds. Ruth C. Duck, and Michael G. Bausch. New York: Pilgrim Press, 1981.

Geoffrion, Jill Kimberly Hartwell. "Thine Is the Power, but What about Mom." *Praying Can Be . . .: Embodied Explorations of the Lord's Prayer.* (Ph.D. diss., 1995.) Cincinnati, Ohio: Union Institute, 1995.

Hong, Edna *Turn over Any Stone.* San Francisco: Harper and Row, 1990.

Lamott, Anne. *Bird by Bird: Some Instructions on Writing and Life.* New York: Anchor Books, 1995.

Merton, Thomas. *Thoughts in Solitude.* New York: Farrar, Straus and Cudahy, 1958.

Miles, Steven. "Imagination and the Care of Demented Persons," unpublished paper, Center for Bioethics, Minneapolis, Minn., 1999.

Nouwen, Henri. *Aging.* Garden City, N.Y.: Doubleday, 1974.

―――. *Out of Solitude.* New York : Walker and Co., 1974.

―――. *Reaching Out.* Garden City, N.Y.: Doubleday, 1975.

―――. *The Way of the Heart.* New York : Seabury Press, 1981.

Wangerin, Walter. *Mourning into Dancing.* Grand Rapids, Mich.: Zondervan, 1992.

Weatherhead, Leslie D. *Salute to the Sufferer.* Bungay, Suffolk, England: Chaucer Press, 1962.

Williams, Charles. *Descent into Hell.* Grand Rapids, Mich.: Eerdmans, 1973.

Suggested Readings

Cohen, Donna, and Carl Eisdorfer. *The Loss of Self.* New York: Plume/Penguin Books, 1986.

Edwards, Jack Allen. *When Memory Fails: Helping the Alzheimer's and Dementia Patient.* New York: Plenum Publishing, 1994.

Feil, Naomi. *The Validation Breakthrough.* Baltimore: Health Professions Press, 1993.

Henderson, Cary Smith. *Partial View: An Alzheimer's Journal.* Dallas: Southern Methodist University Press, 1998.

Hodgson, Harriet. *Alzheimer's: Finding the Words.* Minneapolis: CHRONIMED Publishing, 1995.

Konek, Carol Wolfe. *Daddyboy: A Memoir.* St. Paul: Graywolf Press, 1991.

Mace, Nancy L., and Peter Rabins. *The 36-Hour Day.* Rev. ed. New York: Warner Books, 1992.